Learning to Fish
While
Learning to Live
What a Way to Grow Up

Learning to Fish
While
Learning to Live
What a Way to Grow Up

By

Edward (Bud) W. Larkin Jr.

ISBN 978-1-105-48347-9

Additional Copies:

edcinthlark@att.net

Subject; book

B
Larkins
Lor

Dedication

This book is dedicated to two loving parents, Dorothy and Edward Sr. Thanks, Mom and Dad, for showing me the way and then letting me fly!

Edward W. Larkin Jr.

Preface

I would like to acknowledge the loving understanding of my wife Cindy. I think I drove her nuts as I asked her about parts of this book over and over. My son Chris encouraged me along the way, too, and thanks to son Shaun for pushing me toward the computer skills needed to complete this project. And a tip-of-the-hat to stepson Steve for the inadvertent information on Bantam Lake and the "secret" lures. Lastly, thanks to my friend John Bernetich for being my back-up memory, and a great fishing buddy that hasn't thrown me overboard yet.

Introduction

Maybe it's an autobiography-no, it's about fishing. Maybe it's the story of raising my kids-no, it's about fishing. Maybe it's the story of getting married, or camping-no, it's about fishing.

I enjoy fishing. I guess I love fishing. As I grew up it played a supportive role in all aspects of my life. It intertwined itself with all my stages of development, and gave me time to "come up for air' when things were happy or sad, rough or hectic on life's journey. It smoothed the way, and recharged me along life's path.

I had a feeling one day that it might be good to share some of this interaction, some of my activities, experiences, and adventures with others that may have enjoyed similar circumstances. And maybe there's a chance that someone may see the value of the sport or the importance of taking a kid fishing.

We introduce our youth to all kinds of group sports, but some kids may be inclined to more singular challenges-contests that require planning, patience, and self-reliance. Fishing fits that prescription and there are no outside competitions or umpires involved. Children more than ever need "pressure relief valves". And as a bonus fishing offers a way to develop an appreciation of nature first hand.

There are many magazines and newspapers that support the sport, but there seems to be very few local books. I have enjoyed many of those periodicals, and some have even inspired me to action. But many of us who fish rarely write about our exploits over time. I will try to do as best I can, and hope to show how the sport has supported and, in many ways, enriched me on life's journey. Although I have changed and slowed down (enough to write!), the anticipation and excitement of each "expedition" still exists. I guess it is a lifetime calling.

I am not an author, just a fisherman who wishes to share a few stories. I will do my best to relay my experiences as clearly and as humbly as I can. Hopefully others can see some of themselves in these "ordinary" outings that make life "extra-ordinary" and enjoyable. If I let out any of my secret techniques or special hot spots, please enjoy and don't tell anyone!

Ed (Bud) Larkin Jr.

Contents

Chapter 1

Early Years I:
I Lose My First Big Fish

I don't exactly know when Dad taught me to fish, but I will be forever grateful that he did. I think I was about five or so, and things started out rather simply. Mom would pack sandwiches and snacks, and we would head out to a favorite spot: Lake Garda (my aunt lived there), Bantam Lake, and Batterson Park were all early haunts.

One of the earliest lake trips I can remember was to Bantam Lake. It must have been around 1949 or so. My parents packed up our lunch, and we tried to get a picnic table right near the beginning of Point Folly, close to our favorite spot, facing west and right on the water. Dad tried to get there early but usually had to settle for his second favorite spot, which held significance for me later in life. We would set up, play in the sand, and generally enjoyed the day.

Dad fished some and generally relaxed. I have seen the photos of this, but remember little of this time except for one incident even earlier in my life.

For some reason, my parents, on one outing, got a picnic table out on the far end of Point Folly, near site 19. There is a little stony, sandy, beach area there where one can wade and swim. Being small, my mother carried me into the water to play. She apparently slipped on something and dropped me into the lake! I remember seeing all kinds of beautiful bubbles rising before me. A great commotion took place and I was quickly plucked from the water. I still, to this day, recall those lovely bubbles!

As I said previously, our second picnic table choice was significant. Well, fifty-four years later I met my second wife while country-western dancing and we were married in 1997. I was blown away during our courtship when while walking at Point Folly

I learned that it was her family that got there early enough on a Saturday or Sunday to claim that first prized picnic table! They lived in Thomaston, a much shorter drive and managed to claim their spot early. I remember, at four or five years old, playing with a fishing pole, and being "annoyed" at the girls next to our picnic spot for attracting ducks and tossing bread! They were family of three boys and three girls. *I was trying to fish*! Fish like quiet water, and they were scaring off all my potential catches!

Fifty-plus years later, I married one of those girls! We are still looking for and investigating old photos, but our families were in the same spots at the same time for many trips years ago. Incredible! I guess I did catch something! She was one of the best catches of my life.

Before we discovered Twin Lakes, Dad rented a flat-bottomed wood boat during one of those Bantam Lake outings, and off we went in that rickety vessel with the widow -maker Sear's motor humming us along. We headed for the north bay, the Litchfield side of the lake, and fished the right shore as you look at Sandy Beach. I had a Pflueger Supreme casting reel and a Sears Shakespeare six foot Wonder Rod. I know that because I still have it! I learned to cast with that reel and with the braided nylon twenty-five pound test line.

Using some lure or something I hooked a big fish, and started to play and play it. I got all sorts of advice; "keep the pole up", "no slack", "and keep tension on it"! There was quite a hubbub in that boat and as the fish went by we saw it was a big bass! I coaxed it closer and closer to the boat, Dad grabbed the net and I inched it in. Then the biggest tragedy of my life so far! Mom wanted me to lift it up so she grabbed the rod at midpoint and lifted. Bam – that was the end of that fish as the hook pulled out and the "monster" swam away. Boy was I mad as I tried to hold back a flood of tears and not clobber my mother with the pole. Of course she was sorry and tried to console a kid that didn't want to be consoled. I had lost my first big fish! Dad later thought it was about five pounds, but I thought it was thirty.

The adventure was not over. We fished a bit more, and then started to head in. We had to bail the boat a few times since it was a flat-bottomed boat that leaked a little. We headed west and then south around Marsh Point. The wind had come up and the boat, heading south, began to slap waves. My mother started yelling, as she saw the floor of the boat rippling. We slapped bigger and bigger waves. My little brother and I were scared too, aided by the fact that Mom was becoming a bit screamy! Dad turned around, and went back into the north bay. He had a plan. He dropped us off somewhere on shore and said he would take the boat back alone and we were to walk to the road. It was at that time that I realized that Dad "might die"! I cried and pleaded, but was finally convinced that everything would be okay. I was to help lead everyone out of the "big" woods. We walked for what seemed to be a long way through rough woods with no trail, and ended up on a road somewhere. I guess I was a good guide, and so was my mom because Dad magically showed up somehow, and I remember nothing else. I probably fell into a sleep of relief. Dad was okay, but I was still mad at Mom! What a day, and what an adventure!

Chuckle 1

What a beautiful spread; picking up an unlatched tackle box on a dock!

Chapter 2

Early Years II:
Batterson Park and
West Twin Lake

During those early years, another favorite spot we enjoyed was Batterson Park in New Britain. Our family would park on the north side and cross a big grassy field, carring our poles, worms, peach baskets, tackle boxes, and buckets. Our feet were usually wet by the time we got to the water's edge. We went in the afternoons or evenings, sometimes in the rain or mist. Rainy fishing was always better.

We fished with drop lines. Now, that was an experience. We used nuts, bolts, and Dad's homemade sinkers for weights. We whirled those suckers in circles and let them fly to the water. Well, not always; there is an art to this. Places where there were no fish were trees, straight up in the sky, and just past my brother's ear; not to mention three feet from shore! Then there was the slam in the back of the leg but eventually we learned to hit the lake.

The peach baskets were to sit on. Mom and Dad had umbrellas, but my brother Hal and I were too active for those. Rain; heck, rain doesn't bother kids fishin'.

Dad taught us to hold the line tight and pull when we felt a bite. Eventually we got pretty good at it. We lost a lot of weights there though- hence the use of old nuts and bolts. When those sinkers or weights got stuck, we learned to walk thirty yards or so to the right, then far to the left, pull, pull, pull- climb around trees, up trees, and through bushes trying to free them. If we had no luck, we would get the line as short as possible and pull. Half the time we got our feet wet, and most times we weren't very lucky. Batterson is very rocky, and full of our weights.

Half the fun was exploring, but we were limited by a fence keeping us out of a camp on the northwest side of the lake. In later high school years, I did get to the grassy bank to the south of the camp, and caught a few calicos, a top-secret in our house.

At times there were other fishermen at Batterson too and out of respect for their turf, we kept our distance, Dad's orders.

Mainly we caught bullheads by fishing on the bottom. Those critters were tough, and Dad taught us how to pick them up without getting "pricked", but of course we got "pricked", and we soon learned.

Mom was great. We brought our catches home and we talked her into putting them in the bathtub! Those creatures came alive and fascinated my brother and me. I think I changed the water many times, trying to keep them alive as long as possible, but eventually Dad cleaned them up when Mom couldn't stand it anymore. He gutted them and skinned them while our eyes got wide with wonder.

Another early memory I have involves waiting for opening day. Nothing, except the anticipation of Santa Claus, rivals waiting for opening day. I can remember laying on the top bunk of our bunk bed, my brother Hal on the bottom, and wondering what excitement was ahead the next day. Of course we couldn't fall asleep.

We finally ended up at Greystone's boat livery, located on what we would call "the third lake" at Twin Lakes in Salisbury, Connecticut. We drove in on a dirt, humpy road. The sun was coming up, and I remember the wonderful sounds of crows calling in the trees. The water was mirror like, reflecting trees and the orange sunrise sky. The air was fresh and I was excited as I carefully walked out on the dock with its rumbly boards and exposed nail heads to find our rowboat. That scene is so imprinted on my brain that I have enjoyed it for a lifetime. Thanks Dad!

We fished that lake for perch and bluegills while the beautiful calm, clear water and the spectacle of the bottom moving under the boat mesmerized us. Perhaps I'm still hypnotized today, because I thirst to repeat that happening as often as possible.

Dad casted for those fish with a Pflueger casting reel; and I had a level wind reel, too. I am so glad I learned on a casting reel before I owned a spinning reel. I spent many hours casting that pole in the yard, aiming at cans and bike tires and it taught me patience, I guess, untangling braided line too often to count. We made our lines last for years in those days, since funds were short. Braided nylon was tough and I think several of Dad's tip-ups still have some of that line on their spools. Anyway, during practice, I caught many trees and bushes, and even aimed at my brother a few times! And Dad kept teaching me. The familiar refrain, "Sand will ruin the reel," sang out often. I learned that lesson so well that even now, I don't lay a reel down.

Dad was able to find small bits of scrap metal. He patiently soldered a piece of paper clip to each one and made a mess of sinkers. We rigged those with one or two hooks above, and baited them with juicy night crawler pieces from the critters we caught the night before.

We casted much of the shoreline, and caught many gills and perch this way for a number of years but eventually we graduated to bobbers.

Getting night crawlers was always fun. My first job was holding the light for Dad, but it wasn't long before I was the crawler king! Our yard, as well as our neighbor's yard in Plainville, was blessed with rich soil. Night-crawlering was very productive and it wasn't long before I found out that rainy nights were bonanzas. We never ran out of worms, and Mom always accommodated our coffee cans in the refrigerator. My parents were so wise – what a great way to keep a kid busy.

"Bud," they would say (they nicked-named me "Bud" – i.e. Dad's buddy),"we need more worms for bait!" To this day, I have a hard time straightening up!

For some reason, I don't remember many rides home at this time but Dad would wake our groggy heads up, and we would truck upstairs where we lived. I would head for the bed, and I was out till morning and it must have been peaceful for my parents.

Dad eventually got a small twelve foot wooden plywood boat with a semi-V bottom. It had a deck and a small windshield, and a fifteen hp motor. It was a very modest boat. No! To us it was a yacht. Now we could really get around, especially on Twin Lakes. With my brother and me in the back seat, and Mom and Dad up front, we were the "soup and the nuts"! Now we could explore all of Twin Lakes.

When we went out we ended up on the second or "third" lake because it was safer for a twelve foot boat.

Going under the bridges from the "big" lake was always a great treat. We saw painted turtles and many turtles that looked like rocks. I later learned they were "musk" turtles, and they are no longer there. We also spotted various fish in the spring and those bigger things were bass!

I can remember anchoring in West Twin Lake (Washinee Lake) in ten feet of water or so and watching in amazement as the area under the boat became solid with a stream of perch through which one couldn't see! An almost unbelievable sight it was and I would only see that one more time, in Sodus Bay, New York.

We sure enjoyed those clear mornings on the lake, standing quietly in a slow moving boat as it moved through springtime water. In later years I returned countless times for that experience. Fish here, turtles there, and unanticipated movements everywhere. Add birds, crisp air, and a quiet putt-putt motor (we had no electrics at that time) and you make lifetime scenes that put you peacefully asleep at night.

We probably took more fish than we really needed during this era, but when Dad started cleaning them, we were wide-eyed. In those days, we would lay them out on newspaper, count them, take a picture, and then clean them. Sometimes we had upwards of seventy-two fish, but they fed the family, and we always ate what we brought home – family rule!

Back then I did not like eating fish and that's when I started dipping them in ketchup. Over the years, I finally developed a taste for fish, but I still use ketchup once in a while now too.

Chuckle 2

When a fish breaks water, why are you always sitting untangling line?

Chapter 3

Fair Haven, Lake Ontario

When I was nine or ten, we used to go on vacation to a place called Fair Haven Beach State Park on Lake Ontario in New York. We camped with an umbrella tent, and that campground had platforms, so we stayed dry. There was a great beach, and a long pier to the West, and a river cut right through the beach and filled a lagoon. The pier was the entrance to Sodus Bay, just over a hill. We went perch fishing once out on Sodus Bay in a rented boat with Dad's old outboard and that thing was temperamental. I mentioned this because it was on that trip that I saw a "river" of perch again, big perch, swimming under our boat, covering the bottom completely. I never forgot it; perch, perch streaming along by the hundreds!

Anyway in the evening, we would pack up our stuff, leave the campsite, and go down to the lagoon and fish for what I thought was far into the night. I was just a little kid, so "far into the night" was probably midnight! We fished for giant calico bass from the shore and in this neck of the woods, they called them strawberry bass. Go figure? We had to keep the lines tight and watch for bobber runs – good concentration for a little kid. Light was provided by the Coleman lanterns that each fisherman brought. Anyway, we spent many nights fishing that lagoon, and I am sure other campers wondered why we came back every night so late!

We caught many nice calico, some frying – pan sized, especially near the feeder canal that went past the diving boards. Once in a while, we would get a northern or dogfish, and that caused a real flurry of excitement. We met some nice people doing the same thing, and created lifetime memories while we sat around the lanterns.

It was at this campground that someone told us about camping "on the water's edge" in the Adirondacks. We tried it, and never camped again at Fair Haven, though the memory of that place, with its beach, pier, bay, and lagoon will always have a warm place in my fishing memories. I was eleven when we switched to Adirondack camping, and a whole new world of exciting exploration would fill my life.

Later, in the "Vacations" chapter, I will write about my grandparents who camped at Fair Haven too. It was nice to have a fishing grandpa!

Chuckle 3

How come, just when one needs to go to the bathroom, there are boats everywhere?

My brother Hal and I on the pier at Fair Haven State Park, N.Y., about 1954 (entrance to Sodus Bay).

Chapter 4

Father and Son's Club: Black Pond

When we were very young, maybe eight or ten, Dad joined a group of other men in what was called "The Father and Sons Club". A Mr. Lewis Knox founded it through the YMCA and the church. The men and their sons (Dad, brother Hal, and me) would meet once a month, and go on outings every other month or so.

The "club" consisted of Dad, Mr. Grocki, Mr. Bullard, Mr. Uitz, Mr. Hart, and at first Mr. Knox, of course. Mr. Kohl later joined the group. The idea was to meet, as "Indian guides", and have activities where Dads and sons could share time together. We rotated the meetings at each other's houses. Each father and son would make invitations together, like a small tom-tom, or a tomahawk, and use those invitations to invite others to their house for the meeting. The invitations were hand-delivered to each house. At the meeting the "scribe" would take attendance when the "chief" called the meeting to order and each family had an Indian name. We were the Beavers. The Dads were always called "big" and the child "little". So during the meetings and outings, Dad was Big Beaver, I was Little Beaver, and because my brother was young and "very active", he was called Busy Beaver!

With the jargon the way it is, if we were doing this today, I'm sure we would have picked crow, or bear, or something! I do remember some family was Big Bear, Little Bear; another was Big Wolf, Little Wolf; etc.

The group that we founded later became known as "Indian Guides", an organization in the YMCA and we were the original founding members! Rules were set up, and very soon down the road, the meetings of other groups were held at the "Y" instead of at the homes, although our group still met at folks homes. Eventually, the Indian Princesses for moms and girls was born.

Anyway, one of the greatest activities we did together was a weekend away at "Camp Woodstock" on Black Pond in Woodstock, Connecticut. Camp Woodstock had boats, swimming, a dock, a dining hall, and recreational activities. We would arrive on Friday evening, with the knowledge that we would have to "work" first before we could "play". This was one of our first lessons on "giving back"! Our job (dads and sons) was to scrape the wood boats and caulk them, getting them ready for the season. The boats were old wooden things, upside down on sawhorses and the "kids" had to work all Saturday morning, scraping, caulking, and painting.

We couldn't wait till noon! After a great lunch I headed pell-mell to the water. We usually split up, and some fished, some hiked, some played tetherball but I fished!

To the west of the camp is a big rock and if you could get to it, you had clearance to cast without catching bushes! I fished the rest of the day, trying various spots, and ended up with a stringer of sunnies and bullheads. I remember ending up to the east of the camp, and hitching my stringer to a bush. It was at this time that Mr. Bullard introduced me to the word "hornpout", another name for bullheads or catfish. In later years, I would refer to that name just to get curious looks, telling my friends that I had caught a hornpout.

Anyway, when morning came it brought about another lesson. I ran down to check my great string of fish, and found only heads! Dad followed and I got a lesson on raccoons and turtles.

On other subsequent trips, we were allowed to use the boats, and we paired up as the dads either worked on boats or sat back and "enjoyed". Mr. Grocki's son, Tony, learned how to row in circles, but I finally figured rowing out! There was a girl's camp across the lake, and although some others might have been curious, I was after fish! Girls – yuck! This interest in fishing over girls held for many years and I am sure my parents didn't see any reason to change my direction. That always happens soon enough!

Anyway, straight out across the lake, about two- thirds of the way, we dropped anchor and fished using worms and bobbers. Anyway, we caught nice calico bass, a wonderful find for us and I never forgot that. Mr. Bullard's son, Boyd, was the one who identified these fish. He was a little older, and real savvy on outdoor things.

Boyd was a natural leader and I never saw anyone climb a tree as fast as him. He and a friend, ~~Don~~ Charles Pelletier, would later die tragically, in a spring canoe trip on the upper Connecticut River. They were seniors in high school. What a terrible tragedy and it made a sad and wrenching impression on me. I really looked up to Boyd.

I still have the urge to fish that Black Pond spot today because it's a fine body of water, and I did return once when I was an adult. I caught more good calico and it was an enjoyable little lake. But Black Pond is a long ride and those distances kept me mostly on the western side of the state in the years that followed.

We had great times at Camp Woodstock, running through the woods, fishing and enjoying activities with our dads and friends. The fathers in that "tribe" watched out for the kids. Dad hit a rough patch at this time, contacting hepatitis, and ending up in the hospital for weeks and I can remember waving to him in the hospital window!

The fathers in the club picked up the slack! They took my brother and me on the planned field trips and we visited the Statue of Liberty, and hiked to Eagle Rock in Thomaston, all under the direction of other fathers. I do remember one father saying, "Now I know why they call Hal (my brother) Busy Beaver"! I guess we were a handful?? God bless those dads.

Our tribe eventually discontinued as we got older, but I think all of us were proud to have belonged to the first "Y" Indian Guide group in Connecticut. I will be forever grateful for the times I enjoyed with my dad and the surrogate fathers.

It was quite nice growing up in the late 40's and 50's. We didn't lock our doors. I would hurry home from school, change my clothes (school clothes were special), and "go out and play". If it was raining, there were several options, the last of which was homework. I would head for the attic and do all sorts of projects, or play with my "baseball cards". They weren't all baseball cards of course, some were World War II battle cards, Indian chief cards, round ice cream cup covers with pictures, or famous movie star cards. I won most of them playing "flip" cards or "topsies" against the wall. We played in the rain on front porches, especially Mrs. Tortolani's next-door and we loved it when Mrs. Humbert would give us homemade popsicles. What wonderful neighbors. I can also think back and still hear the music my parents enjoyed on the weekends. I heard Arthur Godfrey's ukulele, the songs of Frank Sinatra, Dean Martin, and Rosemary

Clooney. Dad played Burl Ives "Little White Duck" so much I got tired of it! And what was Christmas without Bing Crosby's "White Christmas" song.

And Dad would teach us a bit about honor and respect. Before each TV baseball game, we would have to stop everything and stand at attention while the national anthem was being played; what a great time.

Back at that time I was asthmatic. I was allergic to cats, dust, hay, – you name it. Dr. Frost, our family Dr., suggested to my parents that I discontinue cows' milk and substitute goats' milk instead. We made contact with a family named Retz, who had goats. They lived near the corner of W. Main St. and N. Washington St. Every week my parents bought goats' milk there, and over the years my asthma disappeared. I was raised on goats' milk and it wasn't bad at all.

Chuckle 4

How come, no matter where you sit in the boat, you get to be anchor man?

Chapter 5

I Get Two Wheels-My
Circle Expands
(Local Ponds)

At some time during the intermediate years, Santa brought me a two-wheeler bicycle. It was a Huffy Convertible! That's some name for a small maroon bicycle, but now I had some range. It wasn't long before I started "exploring" the neighborhood and seeing how many times I could go to the corner and back. Then it became "around the block".

It wasn't long before I was exploring the railroad station and Cronk road that led to the sewer company. It was to the north of Plainville and I eventually knew every nook-and -cranny of that area and of southern Scott Swamp. With the bicycle, my range kept expanding, as my parents slowly loosened the reins. The Pequabuck River ran through this place, and there were a few feeder streams and marshes that were ripe for exploring. To the west was the town dump and I became Swamp Man! I even tried trapping for awhile. Oh, how I began to love marshes. I even built a small hut or hideout in the woods using debris from construction junk stored in the area! Shhhh!

To the north were the Sherman sand piles and a small airport, called Robertson Field. The railroad tracks went directly by both, and continued on over a small stream and past some sand pit ponds in Farmington. Eventually they crossed the Farmington River, which I walked to in high school.

At that time the Paquabuck River was quite polluted but the feeder streams and the sand pits were quite clean. I can remember perching on the roots of a large fallen tree in the spring. I was about seven feet above ground, and watching painted turtles sun themselves in the warmth, just out of "catching" distance. The red - winged blackbirds were singing, and a hawk was working too. Sometimes a muskrat would break the swamp edge in the distance, and mallards were busy looking for food. What a remarkable scene on a Saturday morning and some things just come together in life and imprint themselves in our brains. This was one such thing. I wanted to learn about everything there, lit up in the morning sun and I sat for a long time, just absorbing.

With all these wonderful things stimulating me, I would eventually end up in the library, which was right in my backyard. I looked up things in books and I would eventually read almost every Boy Scout merit badge book they had in the library, as well as nature identification stuff. Now, that's how you stimulate a young boy and I even learned a new word – stalking – and made a green mask out of an old winter pullover hat. Now the animals would never see me! "Swamp Man" became "Invisible Man".

Eventually I got an even bigger bike, a Columbia single speed that got me in pretty good shape!

One of the first places in that swamp I tried to fish was in a little stream that went under the tracks and under Johnson Avenue at the North and of Robertson Airport. Warren, Richie, and I had heard that someone had caught a trout there. You know, that's valuable news!

Off we went, armed with worms, bobbers, and whatever, optimistic as heck. We walked through bushes and sticks, got our feet wet, and probably clobbered the heck out of the place. I caught nothing I can remember but my friend Warren might have gotten a trout. Anyway, we had a great adventure.

On another exploration we went to Hamlin Pond in East Plainville. That pond is the headwater for the Quinnipiac River and Richie's cousin lived pretty close to the place. I soon learned that it was very hard to get to the shore of that lake. In one spot, kids had placed boards to the water's edge. I tried them, and managed to fall off the teetering things and step into knee-deep muck! The whole pond was surrounded by muck and mud, with the accompanying bushes. It was impossible to get close enough to fish it and I learned many years later that when they built the route 72 connector highway, they had to give Hamlin Pond a wider berth than they wanted. The pond was a glacial bore, and the mud was too deep to support a road.

With the amount of times I got mud in my sneakers, I could have told them that!

In any case, the place is alive with turtles and I collected many. I had spotted turtles, painted turtles, and even a small snapping turtle. I buried a big tub (don't know where I got it) in the ground in the backyard and half filled it with water and a rock. I had seven turtles, and fed them well.

However, fate intervened. Connecticut received a near-miss hurricane, and filled my tub with water and when I checked, all my turtles were gone! That ended my collecting.

I began to explore the stream leading out of Hamlin Pond (the Quinnipiac River) and saw places that had access. One spot was near the water company's pump house, and another was where the stream went under Woodford Avenue. Just beyond that was a picturesque millpond with a little dam downstream and those spots looked good.

I returned to these places many times with both my friends and my brother. We fished many hours in those areas, trying to cast under the Woodford Avenue bridge (there were too long tunnels) and caught a few suckers and small bass. We got sunfish near the millpond, and lost hooks and bobbers in the bushes! We spent many hours sitting, talking, and exploring around that bridge-great times!

By this time, I had moved up to a spinning rod and reel. I had the good ol' trusty Mitchell 300 reel. As a matter of fact, I still have several of them, and they still sound, as my friend John says, "Like coffee grinders". Every spring I enjoyed the ritual of taking the thing apart and cleaning and greasing it. Mr. Aivaz, who sold minnows and bait in town, had Mitchell reel parts. Bail springs were quite valued, and I always picked up a few when I could. Joe Aivaz was a wonderful, accommodating man and he could trout fish!

I have to be a little secretive about another area I fished at this time, so keep it under your hat! To the north of the airport were two sand pit ponds. We called them "the Sherman sand pits" and they were clear and nice, and had easy access from the road. On the north side was a big sharp bank leading down to one pond.

My friends and I walked around these ponds many times, casting surface lures. And we found out they held nice big bass. Well, big to us. We hooked several, enough to get us excited. Not much beats the thrill of bass hitting surface lures. As a result we made several trips there until we finally got informed that we were not allowed to fish that property (i.e. we got kicked out).

Not to be deterred, we returned to the second pond sometime later with a plan. Where the steep bank was, we could bullhead fish if we sat down and didn't move much. By sitting down we couldn't be seen, but we could hear the cars go by up behind us. At dusk we had great success and took home a stringer of bullheads! We were pretty proud and planned to do that again sometime, but we never did.

In recent years, WTIC radio located beside the pond, and some employees dubbed it "Lake Solhaney" (sp. ?) after one of their reporters! The western pond where we caught the bass was filled in.

Just a footnote about that western pond; I went back there alone, chasing those bass. I just had to catch them. Remember, swamp man is invisible. I left my bike up the street in the bushes and walked the tracks to the pond. At that time, I had the neatest knife and sheath at my side in case I had to cut bushes, kill bears, or whatever. It had a carved handle and I thought I was Daniel Boone or something. What a neat knife.

Anyway, I started fishing and in no time I saw a truck coming around the other side of the pond. It was security and it was coming fast and I had been spotted. I began to run, south, into the swamp. I could hear I was pursued, so I ran through some mud and junk where I thought no one else would run. It's hard to run full-bore through the bushes with a fishing pole; you have to aim it right! Anyway I was never quite so scared! I didn't want to go to jail or to lose my fishing pole!

Eventually things quieted down and I circled around to my bike and took off for home, dirty muddy clothes and all. My arms were nicked up pretty good too. I arrived home and "karma" had struck. I looked down at my side and my great knife was missing. My first beautiful woodsman knife was gone. It's probably still in that swamp today because I never returned to those sand pits but they sure were wonderful and mystical spots for a young boy to fish!

In that general vicinity, maybe a quarter-mile away, were located the old Nike Missile bunkers. Of course you couldn't go near them, but they eventually closed. Remember "duck-and-cover" exercises in school? Well, a few hundred yards behind those bunkers we located a pond; I was always exploring. During the winter, we decided to ice fish the place and we traveled on foot from home. We came in from the back, and set up several tip-ups.

My friends, Warren and Richie, were there and we had our usual fun. At some point, I had a flag! After great commotion, we pulled a humongous bass through the ice. Now, if you want to see boys dance that would have been the time. A big fish came from a *very* small pond. That fish went home and weighed in at about five pounds and another wonderful memory was planted in my life! We had a ball that day. We walked in the snow for what seemed like several miles to get to that place. We had all our gear and junk but learned a lesson: big fish can come from small ponds! And fishing had made us a little tougher and happier and hard work did pay off.

Chuckle 5

Why does a fish jump elsewhere, just *after* you cast?

Chapter 6

Other Places You're Not Supposed to Go

There were a couple of other places where one wasn't supposed to fish so I checked them out!

One summer during this time, I had obtained a two-man pup tent. What a great piece of equipment with a screened window in one end, and screening at the entrance. It also had a sewn in floor. I set it up in the backyard, and my parents let me try it out (eventually that tent would get to Manitoba).I was pleased with the tent. Then my brain began to whirl, and I figured out that I might be able to fish at night – i.e. sneak out!

I had checked out a pond on Cooke Street named Paderewski Pond. It was privately owned or something, because one couldn't go in there to fish for the big bass that were supposed to be there. There were rumors at school about those fish and I saw them – huge bass breaking water! Anyway, by way of maps and exploring, I found a back way into the place on Grant Avenue. As this was reachable by bike, I made secret plans to run an expedition there.

I got my pole and lures together, especially my black jitterbug, and placed my bicycle close by beside the house. The night was warm, and I got "permission" to sleep in my tent! I watched, I watched, and after what seemed like forever, the lights went out in the house, and off I went!

Paderewski of course looks different at night, spooky and silent, except for an occasional strange sound here and there. I snuck in anyway via Grant Avenue and scrambled into some pines. The moon was fairly bright, coming up in the east, and it was cool and clear. I was on the west side, found an opening and made a few casts; to the right, to the left, nothing! "What gives?" I thought.

Well it didn't take long for a little fear, and even more guilt for sneaking out, to take over. I was soon home again in my tent, frustrated that those "big" bass didn't hit. It wasn't until sometime later that I learned Paderewski Park had a great abundance of carp! And I'm pretty sure that's what rolled on the surface when I identified them as bass on earlier scouting trips. That pond has bass but I never caught any.

It was about this time in my life that I discovered geological survey maps. It might have been my friend Warren that put me onto them, but they just grabbed my attention and were the "Google maps" of the time.

I sent away for information and order forms, and ordered a few local maps. When they came, I was impressed. Now I could find little-known ponds and streams all over the place! There was a steep learning curve and I really studied those things. I still have a tendency to collect maps today.

One of my favorite places to hang out was in our attic. Attics are beautiful places. Our attic, my "center of operations", allowed me to do many activities. Besides studying maps, I built model antique cars. Remember the great model hobby shops? One would go in and the shelves would be lined up with all kinds of things to be glued and snapped. I bought a few cars over time and had great fun piecing and gluing them together. I even bought one of those balsam airplanes that come in a box and look like flat pieces of wood. Using a razor knife and a sharp eye, I cut all those tiny pieces out and put together an airplane, ribbed wings and all. It took forever but I never did put the "skin" on the plane, I guess I lost interest. The thing still exists, along with some model cars, hanging in my parent's attic!

Still in the attic also is the Lionel train and home- made 6 x 10' table Dad built for us. We had roads, trees, houses, buildings, and landscapes all set up and running. The old black engine smoked out of the stack when you dropped the pellet in, and the Santa Fe engine ran on a separate track. That train table separated my end of the attic from my brothers, and we had great "trips" on those trains!

I also had my trusty chemistry set all set up and unfolded on an old door I had used as a counter. Boy, some of those concoctions really stunk! What a great way to learn to read and follow directions and I loved the test tubes.

I remember being a naïve kid, thinking I could pull off a fast one. Remember Zarex, an orange liquid one could put in water, like

Kool-Aid, to make drinks? Well, I put some in one of my test tubes, corked it, and made my way up town to Thrall's Drugstore. Now Thralls had a soda fountain at that time, and we could ask for a glass of seltzer for free. They had great ice cream floats, but seltzer was free. Well, old smarty me ordered seltzer, and had a small sip. When no one was looking, the test tube was uncorked and in went the Zarex. Add an old Popsicle stick for a stirrer, and I had a drink.

Pretty smart eh-and naïve! You know, Mr. Thrall was a nice man, as I think back. Not a word was said, and he seemed to smile a lot. And I never got caught!

Anyway, I scrounged up (I was a great scrounger) some old window shades and stripped off the shade part. I was able to staple my maps to the wooden shaft and hang them from the roof rafters in that attic. I had pull-down maps!

The attic was my place for seclusion and experimentation and things got done and planned there. For the chemistry experiments I tried to put a sink in place – a tin can with a bucket. My brother set up his operations in the other end of the attic and we each had a little window.

Several experiments didn't go well. One of our operations involved a string, a big bolt, and an open window. We tied the bolt to a long string and tied the other end to a pipe. We opened the little window, and for some reason wanted to see what would happen if we threw the bolt out of the window – string attached. Well something happened all right! We were on the third floor and just under us was the second floor picture window, and Mom and Dad relaxing in front of the living room TV. Yup! The bolt got to the end of the string, and came back acting like a grenade through the picture window. To say all hell broke loose would be a bad understatement. Damn kids! And we were trapped – no place to run!

At another time, we tried some experiment with an alcohol Bunsen burner type thing. Hal and I were in our PJs in the evening and after lighting the burner we knocked it over. Alcohol started burning on the table and on my brother's bathrobe. The fire was dripping off the table, too! I stripped his robe off and beat out the fire with his bathrobe. Lucky-a fire in an old attic-you bet we were lucky! We were both shaken to the core, and never mentioned it to anyone. We also never used fire in the attic again! Thank you Lord!

I began to discover more ponds on my maps. Just behind the high school and within bicycle distance was a pond located on Tomlinson Avenue. A bike ride soon confirmed the find, but it was posted!

After some research and asking around, I found out that a lady who watched out over that place; a) had a shotgun and, B) didn't like intruders and would use the gun! Of course this was all speculation, rumor, conjecture, and hearsay – but one had to be careful. I went in one day anyway. I had heard about big pickerel, so my pole and my daredevil lure made the trip. I made my approach along a line of pine trees and set up for casting. It wasn't long before I saw a large pickerel follow-up my cast. About the same time, someone was coming, some lady to my left. I never looked back! I scrambled home, and never entered that property again, but I did start some nice "stories" about the giant fish that probably still lived there.

My maps sent me in yet another direction. To the west was a pond (now) called Malone's Pond. It was in Forestville, but still within bicycle range.

On a fine spring Saturday, I collected my pole, bobber, and worms and took off for Forestville. I found a good spot along the road and casted out my bobber but something caught my attention. There were these very, very little frogs around. I don't remember how, but I caught a bunch of them, and was fascinated by how small they were – little fingernail size. Anyway, I managed to catch two trout; yep, my very first trout. And they were pretty nice! I had a good Saturday!

I had the frogs in my worm jar and two trout on a stick and headed home. I was pretty happy with the turnout.

When Dad saw the fish he was curious. The trout turned out to be speckled trout! I believe they were the only two speckled trout I ever caught. And the frogs- I looked them up in my trustee collection of Golden outdoor books and found out they were spring peepers! And I had caught them. To this day I hear them all over the place on my walks but can't seem to even see them, much less catch them. Ain't youth wonderful! Anyway, I didn't get kicked out of that place.

Chuckle 6

This information I hate hearing; "They were biting good yesterday"!

Chapter 7

We Discover the Farmington River

I love Saturdays! We had a great bakery in town – Roger's Bakery – and they had the best cookies and filled doughnuts "in the world"! My brother and I would often swing by there on Saturday morning to ask for "broken ups". Now, broken ups are doughnuts, cookies, and other pastries that were broken and were hard to sell. Sometimes they were just one-or-two-days-old stuff. We must have looked like forlorn waifs, because we were rarely disappointed.

For five cents, the lady behind the counter would give us a bag of broken ups that included cookie parts, stale filled doughnuts, crawlers broken in half, and if we were lucky, individual-sized square apple or pineapple pies! Wow!

Now our landlord's property butted against our apartment property, and included a big red barn and two large compost bins. I would head behind the bins and, in secret, consume my broken ups. I think my mother finally caught on as to why we were not very hungry for lunch on Saturdays.

As time went by, I deduced that I needed spending money. Somehow, I put together a shoeshine kit, and got tips from other guys that were doing the same thing. Shining shoes was a popular way to earn some cash then! I got some rags and cleaning polish, some waxes, an applicator brush, a polishing brush, and a "snap" rag and headed out to find a good location. After trying a few spots, I located myself – yup – in front of the bakery! I got a few customers but was disappointed with the little profit I was making.

So I started to think – where are there more shoes. Then an a-ha moment! We had a bowling alley down the street. It was a duck- pin place a block away, and I decided to go there. The bakery and the grocery store across the street didn't seem to pan out.

I asked the owner if I could shine shoes at the lanes, and he set me up in a little corner of my own, but I couldn't call out "shine, shoeshine" anymore. To my pleasant surprise business got brisk. Men were dropping off their shoes after putting on their bowling shoes and walking away. I shined and shined, and ended up with a problem. I didn't know who belonged to which shoes, and I began to get flustered and worried. I had to be home at a certain time and the owner asked me not to bother the bowlers. I was in a pickle and to me this was a crisis!

With my tail between my legs, I went to the manager. With a not too happy expression on his face, he had to carry the shoes around for people to identify. I was paid, and exited the building, and was asked to not come back. My shoeshine business fizzled and I was too embarrassed to return anyway. Lawn mowing was next. After all, I still needed money for lures and line.

Either on one of those great Saturdays, or in the summer, my friends and I headed out on another fishing trek. I had two great fishing buddies, Warren Muller and Richie Roman. We were the "Three Musketeers" and over time became close as brothers.

We started walking from my house to the railroad tracks north of town and headed straight north toward Farmington. We knew (and my maps confirmed it) that the tracks crossed the Farmington River. That River held fish!

We harassed and bonded with each other all the way-three boys rambling on a warm, sunny day. One of many memorable excursions we would enjoy in our youth.

After about a five mile walk we came to the big bridge that crossed the river. Now my friend Warren was afraid of heights but I loved heights and wanted to be a pilot, or so I thought. Anyway, Richie and I, after much pleading and encouragement, very carefully walked Warren across the bridge, one careful step at a time, asking him not to look down between the beams that held the rails. The river flowed far below.

We fished for a few hours, and didn't catch much, maybe a dace or a sucker or two, but had good fun. We walked Warren back over the bridge, and I got a stupid idea; kids do that you know! I was going to tease Warren. I headed back to the bridge, ran out on it, scrambled under it and did a few chin-ups from the bottom of the bridge. Warren got quite upset, so I quit and we started home, no more teasing. It was stupid anyway!

We all tried walking on the track itself, like a balance beam, and Richie and Warren went as far as they could. When I got on, I found I had good balance, and walked all the way home without falling off. That's a long way. This balance thing became both a blessing and a curse. My sensitive balance caused me to get both carsick and seasick. Farther down the road, I painted houses part-time for over twenty years and never fell off a ladder. I guess one takes the good with the bad!

We would later drive our bicycles to the center of Farmington and fish the river there, but we still had much to learn. Trout don't like high sun in the middle of summer!

Another fishing tip I picked up was that there were fish in the stream that led out of the fish hatchery in Southington. I think it was called Dewey Brothers fish hatchery or something. Anyway, I biked all the way there by myself and found only a trickle of a stream heavily covered by branches and brambles. The trip was a bust.

I did investigate the Quinnipiac River down by the Patten Brook Dairy on several of my summer excursions, but never remember catching much. The river was hard to get to with all the summer underbrush.

On another trek, I went to New Britain in search of Loon Pond. When I found it near New Britain Ave., at the top of a hill, it was only half-full and muddy. It wasn't fishable and it was later drained for a quarry.

Chuckle 7

This I can't figure out: when you buy a dozen minnows, everything hits; when you buy three dozen minnows, nothing hits!

Chapter 8

Bicycle Hikes: Satan's Kingdom/Black Rock Park

Our range with the bicycles got much bigger. Sometime in early high school, Warren, Richie, and I decided to go on an ambitious fishing trip, bicycling to Satan's Kingdom on the Farmington River in New Hartford. I had passed by there many times with my parents, because this was the route we took to Compensating Reservoir and Twin Lakes.

Richie came over to my place to pick me up, and we strapped our tackle and lunches to our bikes and carried our poles as we headed to Broad Street where Warren lived. Richie had one of those "fancy" bicycles with the handle grips for brakes. I don't know how it happened, but as with all accidents, it happened fast. Going down Broad Street, Richie must have hit a rock or a stick or something and the front brake at the same time. Yup! There he went, ass over teakettle over the front handle bars, rolling like tumbleweed down the sidewalk.

He looked pretty dazed, as he got up half surprised, half confused, and half mad (figure that one out!),and a bit embarrassed. Quietly mumbling and muttering and pretty disheveled, he climbed back on, a hard "brake" lesson learned, and we continued on to Warren's house.

Now Warren's mom, Clara, was like a second mother to me. She was interested in our activities, and baked the best cookies. She was a good sport and we enjoyed our visits with her. I knew she also communicated with my mom, so I was always aware of a caring watch! And Warren's father, Wilbur, had a great sense of humor. He always had a joke, sometimes a very dry joke, at the ready. He always had a smile for us, and would sometimes laugh more at his jokes than we did.

After Warren's mom checked out Richie and added a few Band-Aids, we left on our happy way for one long bicycle ride. It was about fifteen miles as we went up route 177, through Unionville, Collinsville, to route 44 in Canton. We stopped and checked the river out in various locations, but kept plugging away till we reached our destination. We were a bit pooped, but fished for several hours, and caught nothing very impressive. The river and surroundings seemed awesome enough, and we were proud of reaching our destination. I think Warren caught a trout or two as he was the premiere trout person amongst the three of us.

Eventually we started home. Warren and I were up front and Richie was third when we came to the junction of 177 and 44. When Richie turned the corner, we heard some sort of verbiage and turned to see him stopped. As we approached him, we learned that his line had been slowly slipping off his reel and was trailing hundreds of feet back. At his expense, of course, we had a great laugh, as he slowly figured out how to reel all that line back in. He was lucky no car had run over it as it trailed far into the distance.

That was one of many wonderful episodes we would have over the following years, playing a lot of sandlot basketball, trading lures, cruising around, and fishing whenever and wherever we could. Fishing buddies are one of the great collections of life, and as good friends we seemed to stay focused on our shared sport.

My parents were always great campers, and as a result, I became familiar with Black Rock State Park in Watertown, Ct., and another idea took root!

Somehow, Richie and I decided to go camping. I had a tent and we had bicycles. Why not? We talked our parents into granting us written permission, bundled up our stuff, and took off!

We went through Forestville, then Bristol, into Terryville, and finally into Plymouth. Terryville and Plymouth were tough, because there was a lot of uphill, pushing bikes and equipment. We had the tent, canteens, sterno, a pan or two, blankets, etc. Our reward, camping and fishing, waited at the other end and a big downhill, Plymouth Hill, loomed just ahead.

Sometimes you don't know it as a kid, but the good Lord watches out for us somehow! Down we started, picking up speed. We were in a semi-controlled downhill plunge, break-necking our way to the bottom when we whizzed through some road construction crew half way down. Boy, did we get yelled at. "SLOW DOWN!" and some other unintelligible words streaked by us as we raced to the bottom. We slowed down quite a bit and those fellows probably saved our skins. Good Karma?

Anyway, we passed through Thomaston and finally got to the park. We rode up to register for a campsite and had trouble, trouble, trouble. We weren't adults, not even sixteen yet. But, but, but---we had our permission slips and it was time for some pleading and negotiating. We were too pooped to bicycle the many miles back home, and it was mid afternoon.

Time for a phone call! The chief ranger, whoever he was, called my mom, and glory-be, we were able to stay. What a break! We got a lecture that went something like—"I'm not supposed to do this," and "You're under my care," and we got the impression that,only through the goodness of his heart, we could stay!

We knew we better behave, and really appreciated this man's goodness in letting us camp overnight. He set us up in kind of a private area under some pines, off by ourselves. I think his cabin had a window facing us.

Anyway, we set up camp, checked out the pond and stream, but didn't catch fish for supper. Good thing we had Dinty Moore beef stew, ready to heat in the can.

We made a campfire and rested that evening, and with our heads against a log, peered at the stars, and talked about the universe, our beliefs, and what not. We sure were trying to make sense of the world. It was a great time for two young kids, thanks to a wise and trusting ranger!

The next day, we packed up and made our way home. The trip home was uneventful, but the whole excursion has always stayed with me. We were a bit too tired to fish much and we tried for trout, but caught nothing I remember. We did make great memories that have priceless value.

Chuckle 8

Ever get frustrated when you have two bobber poles out, and you pull the wrong one when the bobber goes under!

Chapter 9

I Get a Job
(In other words:Lures!)

Money's always nice to have – especially when you're a kid! Aside from the tooth fairy, or returning deposit bottles, it was hard to come by.

Our landlord was Mr. Dick Minor and his wife was Mary Gibbon Minor. They were the most gracious, caring people in the world. My great grandfather used to work for Mr. Minor's father way back when the barn was used for horses and there was a big garden between our apartment and the Minor house.

Anyway, Dick and Gibbon Minor watched Hal (my brother) and I grow up. They were tremendously important and supportive during those years and gave us our first jobs. We became snow shovelers.

As children, we were always instructed to "not play in Mr. Minor's yard," and "that's not our yard, stay out of there" became a familiar theme drilled into us. So it became fascinating when my parents were asked if Hal and I could shovel their walk. Of course, my parents gave us the okay and we had dollar signs in our eyes! I must say, we did a good job. I don't know why, but most snowstorms seemed to come at night and my mother would wake us up at 4:30 AM or so and get us out the door to shovel. As we short-cutted on our way through our landlord's backyard of snow draped apple and butternut trees, we couldn't help but pause. We listened to the silence. It was dark and awesomely fresh enough to make even a child stop with wonder. We finally got to cut through the Minor yard, and we shoveled. We made six or seven dollars each and thought we were rich. Eventually, as the years went by, I ended up shoveling not only their walk, but our walk, Mr. Humbert's walk, and Mrs. Tortolani's walk next-door. This went on for many years, even after I was married. Eventually I used a snow blower, but it seemed I took care of half the neighborhood.

Now I had some funds, and I took up sending for catalogs. By this time, I had my own tackle box, and was eager to fill it! Those catalogs and the local hardware and "box" stores of the time carried various lures and tackle to be desired.

And so it was that both my friends and I started collecting. Unfortunately, I haven't stopped yet. One of my favorite stores was Myrtle Mills of Unionville. They had the greatest tackle selection on the basement floor, and that's where I would head when my parents would shop.

As time went by, the Minors hired me to be their yards man and I learned how to mow the lawn and pull weeds – many, many weeds. Mr. Minor loved gardening, and had upwards of twenty-five flowerbeds in his yard. I became the "gardener" and relieved Henry (who was their longtime master gardener) of many of his duties. He eventually retired and passed away, but between Mr. Minor and Henry, I got a whole education about gardening that is valuable to me to this day.

One such lesson that really impressed me was when a big metal clothesline pole was placed in the ground with a pulley on top. It was heavy – four guys put it up. But the pulley ended up facing the wrong way. Take it down? No. Ask Henry. Henry placed a heavy rope around the middle of the pole and made a tourniquet with a big stick. He then turned the huge pole, right in place with the stick.

I listened to Henry more intently after that, quite impressed with his wisdom. He was old, and he would sometimes fall asleep in the driveway in his black '52 Chevy. He was considered grumpy, and other kids were of frightened of him but I think it was an act, to keep kids out of the yard. He was very kind to me.

Now, as my friend Warren started collecting lures too, he came across a company called Herter's, and ordered all kinds of nice things from there. He eventually got into making his own poles and tying his own flies. I must say, his Grey Ghosts and Mickey Finns were better than store-bought, and during the high school years we more than once limited out at Twin Lakes on his lures. To this day I still have some of his great "ties" and one of his fly rods.

His son, Matt, would eventually tie flies, too, and worked in a tackle store in West Yellowstone, Montana, tying for retail and mail-order.

And so it was that my lure and tackle collection expanded. On one of those Fair Haven – Lake Ontario visits, I remembered my grandfather (Grandpa Larkin) casting a Creek Chub Pikie Minnow. I got several of those and a few L&S Mirror Lures too.

The collection grew, and over these years companies like Heddon, Creek Chub, Eppinger, Arbogast, and a few mongrel companies commanded my wallet. And with each new arrival by mail, my interest and collection grew. Now, sadly, some of these lures ended up (I would like to say, bitten off, but that's not true) in the bottom of the lake or decorating some tree or bush far out of reach. I was always amazed and perplexed that a spoon could go so far when it is snapped off casting. Such is life.

I gradually reined in my spending over the years. Reluctantly, going to college and romance took priority, not to mention raising kids. However, in the spring, I do lose a bit of command to Bass Pro and Cabela's! Habits die hard.

Some of the best times I've had are "sessions" with my friends Warren and Richie, haggling and trading lures. Now, this is one of the best ways to get lures without money.

We would empty our tackle boxes on a table (mostly at my friend Warren's house) and discuss every detail of every lure, emphasizing and praising the attributes of those lures we wanted to give up. You never saw lures with such attributes. And the lures we would find beside the lake or in a bush were just fantastic! One never saw such "hornswaggling" in your life. Of course none of us were buying each other's stories.

After those many hours, we would load up our boxes and go home, and usually any trades that took place were usually "bad lures for bad lures" kind of a deal. But they had potential. If you wanted a good lure, it would take at least three bad ones to get it.

I still have some of those old, beautiful lures today. They're retired, like me, but I'm not ready to release them from my custody yet.

Chuckle 9

It's kind of fun to watch fisherman in another boat cast like crazy when your snapped off spoon lands on the other side of them.

Chapter 10

The Kayak

Once we started camping in the Adirondacks, we camped right on the water's edge. Then something caught my eye. While looking through one of the popular fishing magazines, I saw an advertisement for a Dedham kayak kit. Yep, I could build my own boat. I had started working around age twelve, weeding and mowing, so I was able to buy lures, reels, and so forth. It wasn't long before I had the money for a kayak kit and I sent for it.

It came, and what a letdown because it looked like a box full of sticks and canvas, and a couple quarts of something? Well, after the confusion wore off, I wasn't deterred, and after reading the directions a hundred times, I began. I built the thing right in the backyard, leaving it out each night. Progress was fun!

It took quite a while, but gradually the form started coming together. My parents were a great help, too. Gently bending sticks and using screws and glue the skeleton was finally completed and then the learning curve got steep; canvas and dope? Yes, the stuff that covered airplanes was to be used for the kayak. That's what the two quarts of stuff was about.

I used to lie in the grass at the Plainville airport and dream of being a pilot. Eventually I got to see the piper cubs up close, and even snuck in a few to pretend I was flying. I was surprised at how they were covered with only a hardened type of canvas. Well the kayak had to be covered the same way and with Dad's help, after tacking the white canvas to the frame, we painted on the dope stuff and "voila!" a hard shell took form.

We had wonderful neighbors. Mr. Humbert, Mrs. Minor's brother, lived in the front brick house and saw my project. He seemed to have concern on his face. After hearing my great plans for my kayak, he left. He returned the next day and with a big smile, he presented me with a brand new super-duper life jacket. That was so special that to this day I remember it, and over the years realized how concerned he was for my safety. Great neighbor! Great friend!

That kayak got used in Twin Lakes, especially in the "second" lake, West Twin. I fished for bass mainly, and had a ball with surface stuff. My lure fascination grew, as did my love of exploring "just around the corner".

My parents were so wise and trusting. What a great way to keep me out of trouble. We took the thing camping, too, to the Adirondacks where I had great experiences exploring lakes and the Fish Creek stream. One could go from lake to lake by boat, and I sure did. In those years I was one of the first with a kayak while most people had canoes at that time.

In the mountains on one of my first exploration trips with that kayak, I went through several small ponds to a stream named Spider Creek. This creek connected the campground ponds with a lake called Follensby Clear Pond. I say "lake" because in New York, a "pond" can be a mile long! It was about five or six A.M., and the area was customarily foggy. I wanted to fish the small tiny creek with a surface lure, and started to troll it behind the slow moving kayak. Now this stream is only about thirty feet wide, with a three- foot bank on the west side and as I slowly paddled, I started hearing noises, like leaves rustling, following me along the shore. I stayed alert as I moved upstream but was getting very nervous. Something was in the woods! As I went a little farther, a blue heron in front of me flew from a perch in a low tree. Then a loud "scream" rang out that stood my hair up! Without pulling in any pole, I paddled like there was life on the line and got out of that creek. I could hear my heart in my ears for quite a while.

I fished in the lake for a few hours and after the sun came out and people began to stir, I made my way back through the creek and headed to camp.

After I relayed my harrowing tale to other campers, and a consensus was reached. Their conclusion was that I had disturbed a bobcat stalking a heron for breakfast. When "breakfast" flew away, the bobcat let me know his displeasure. I stayed clear of Spider Creek on early mornings for many days after that.

At another time, Dad was asked by a camping neighbor to go bass fishing. I wanted to go, but he said no. They went to the same

Follensby Clear Pond, and fished most of the day. So, I went in my kayak myself! As long as I wore my life jacket, I was given a long "leash". What better way to tire a kid out on vacation than to let him paddle his brains out.

Anyway, off I went, a hula popper on my pole, and hope in my heart; a little mad that Dad could not take me with him. And did I have success! I came proudly home with five bass on my stringer. I had fished the lily pads and the shadows. Dad and friends returned later, and they got skunked. Talk about a boy beaming! I had out fished three adult fishermen and was excited. I proudly showed off my catch tied to our homemade dock and of course this story was repeated by the campfire many times over the years. Dad and Mom would just smile.

I later finally sold the kayak for a nominal price to my friend, Warren's brother Johnny Muller, who took it down the Farmington River. It got messed up on some rocks by what is now Apricot's Restaurant. He fixed it up, and I lost track of it from there. I was soon to get my own boat, but the kayak gave me the taste of floating freedom, and the genie was out of the bottle.

For years after this, surface lures were in charge of my fishing attention. And I still get excited seeing bass crash the surface for floating enticements. The early years imprinted that on me pretty well, and it is one of my favorite forms of fishing.

Chuckle 10

Why does the BIG fish get hooked on the day you forgot the net??

My homemade kayak!

Chapter 11

I Get a Boat

As I mentioned earlier, I started working in earnest at age twelve; weeding, gardening, and mowing after school. I also mentioned before that Dad got the twelve foot boat with the wooden ribs and plywood bottom. It had a small wooden deck with the fifteen-horse Evinrude on the back and the thing even had a steering wheel.

We started making trips to Twin Lakes for those gills, perch, and bass if we could find them. I remember when we first got the "yacht" Dad was delighted with the speed. At Twin we went to the second lake, then under the third bridge to what we called the "third" lake to try the boat. It was a nice cruise for a family of four.

But Dad wanted to see just how fast he could go. As I think back, he was young at that time, too. So, he put my mother, my brother, and I on the east shore (there were no cottages there at that time) so we could watch, and he took off to the center of the lake and went back and forth! He had a splendid cruise, and he went *fast*.

As he turned toward shore to pick us up, he was still coming rather fast and something happened. Dad quickly turned, went up on the shore, flew into the bush tops, and went out again into the lake. He killed the motor while Mom let out a bit of a scream! It was something to see a boat doing a "U" turn on the tops of bushes!

What happened? As it turned out, one of the rings that held the steering cables pulled out of the old wood, causing major steering problems. Dad came sheepishly to shore, a bit pale and dazed, glad that the boat was still intact! And after being airborne, he putt-putted around the rest of the time.

Now that old boat leaked and I got a good lesson in boat repair. Dad decided to fiberglass the bottom of the boat and we turned it over in the yard and had it on sawhorses of some kind. We sanded the bottom of the boat, got it prepped, and laid the fiberglass cloth over it. Next we mixed the resin with the hardener.

As I remember, that was tricky. One coat of the stuff wasn't working well, and came out a bit sticky. It also had bad fumes and I remember Dad got dizzy as hell. Anyway, on the second coat the color blue was added to the resin and it was quickly applied. He had to work fast, because it hardened fast. The boat came out fine when all was done, and I marveled at the paint brush sticking up in this can of solid glass, hard as a brick.

The boat never leaked again, and it was never lightweight again either. But good times were had and Twin Lakes became a favorite haunt. When we went on vacation up north, I learned to ski behind that boat, with a fifteen-horse motor. We were just light kids. Talk about "hard to get up"!! We quickly learned to be pulled off a dock, to avoid plowing water.

So we had a little runabout boat and a kayak now. Fishing more and more dominated my plans, and by the age of fourteen, I wanted my own boat. Why not! After all, I had a job, and I was making $4 to $6 a day pulling weeds and gardening, and my hours kept increasing.

I started collecting information and catalogs, and studied up on things. I don't know how I was introduced to the place, but Keller's Marine was just to the east of Plainville, in New Britain. Probably that was where Dad got the fiberglass stuff for his boat. They sold the Starcraft brand of boats, and I spotted one I liked in no time, and started saving money. I suppose I drove my parents "nuts", but eventually we returned to Keller's to buy a boat!

Now, this is the way it was set up. The twelve foot aluminum boat (with teak wooden seats) and trailer cost a whopping $170. Somehow, I bought it on credit using my father's name! I was to make payments of seven dollars a month until it was paid off. I even had a payment book. No problem. I was about fifteen now, and was soon to have my driver's license, too. Could you believe my luck!

Such wise parents, huh? I was busy working, had responsibility, and paid that boat off in no time. When I wasn't working, I was waxing or fussing with my beautiful boat. You can't imagine how many fish I caught, sitting in the yard in my boat! I was growing up.

That boat is now over fifty-three years old and has been everywhere. I still have it, and it may be destined for my grandson or granddaughter. My nick- name was Bud and everyone knew me by that name. I was Dad's buddy when I was born so that name stuck and the boat's name became "Bud's Buddy". And it certainly has been that!

That boat has been trailered or car-topped to about every lake that I have ever fished. It's been out west to Manitoba, to Lake Ontario, the Thousand Islands, and of course to the Adirondacks. If there was a memory chip in the boat, it would be a book itself! And it's paid for itself a thousand times over.

Sitting in the warm sun, drifting, trolling, or still fishing still beckons me. And a favorite activity that is always coupled with fishing is exploring. New lakes and places are always calling and boating is a great way to answer that call.

Chuckle 11

Why, after de-hooking a fish, do you throw the pliers overboard instead of the fish??!

My "Bud's Buddy" boat.

Chapter 12

Twin Lakes-Here I Come (I Get My License)

As my lure inventory expanded, so did my circle. I got my driver's license and fishing license. My boat, my friends, and I began to get around.

Dad had a Plymouth with those "stylish" fins that popped up in the back, and a push button transmission. No matter, it had a hitch.

During high school, Warren, Richie, and I would end up at Twin Lakes almost every weekend, especially in the spring; three kids in a twelve foot aluminum boat! No matter, we all could swim, and remarkably, we never had a problem.

I had been working for Mr. Minor, our landlord and friend, now for four years. He had a house at Sachem's Head in Guilford, CT., and I had also worked for him there. He knew I had a boat, and low and behold, he had a five horsepower Johnson outboard motor in storage sitting in his garage on a stand. It was a wine colored beauty and to my delight, he asked if I would be interested in borrowing it. I was elated and quickly said yes.

He kindly showed me how to use it, how to mix the gas with the oil in the six gallon pressurized tank, and to my house it went. I used that 1957 motor for hours on end, and for years. I took care of it better than anything I had. I didn't even trailer it on the boat, but would put it on at the lake. I always returned it to him every fall, winterized, and every spring he would let me use it again. What a man – he never used that motor again – never asked for it back! That family's generosity had a tremendous effect on me and our family!

So, as the "three musketeers" made countless trips to Twin Lakes, we went through a giant learning curve. We first tackled bass and our first success was the good old Hula Popper! We casted and popped that thing on every shoreline possible, and had some pretty good success. Twitch, twitch, pop, pop, splash! We started catching fish. The Jitterbug and Crazy Crawler didn't seem to work as well, especially during the day, but at least we had them in the box if needed. We had great success on the north shore of the big lake, to the right of the launch, and in numerous places in the second lake, West Twin.

And the competition!! One lure would land, and the next one would land about a foot ahead. Warren and I would "battle" to cast to the next good spot while poor Richie ended up on the middle seat. But, he had a plan. He would fish toward the middle of the lake, in the opposite direction (like he had a choice) and more often than not, he too would catch fish. For some reason, he had more "birds' nests" (great humongous tangles) than us, but we had our share too. And those Mitchell 300 reels just kept on grinding!

Our knowledge base and skill level improved over time, and we lost fewer lures to the trees and bushes. We also mastered some knots, even learning how to snell hooks. Eventually we also went to heavier line, since lures cost money. We became extremely adept at ducking missile-like lures when they came out of a tree or off the water after a great yank!

We discovered techniques and more lures too. We settled on a Midge-oreno and the Creek Chub Darter for a time, and found out that if one worked the Midge-oreno really, really fast just underwater, the bass would sometimes nail the thing. What a thrill!

We also fished for pickerel and calico bass, especially in West Twin Lake. We would troll Daredevils and Cobra spoons and do quite well when we skirted the weed beds. Then we gave the Flatfish a try, and found out that it was dynamite on calico and sometimes other fish. We even got trout on them. We would troll back and forth along the western shore of the second lake and have great success with F5 frog and the F7 natural scale model. And there was always someone who would throw out a Daredevil or Cobra spoon to troll and the speed was never right! Either the Flatfish lure was going too fast, or the spoon was going too slow and picking up weeds. We never could find the right combination. And as good friends, and as stubborn as we were, we never killed each other over it either.

For a while, we mainly fished West Twin (Washinee Lake), staying out of the way of those bigger boats and "professional" adult fishermen. We loved the calm and clarity of the place, and the scenery to this day is rejuvenating! Nothing compares to gliding through glassy water, in the shallows, sunshine on your back, and watching the weedy bottom slip by. Fish would dart here and there, all sizes, and an occasional turtle would sprint away. If we were lucky, we would see a "big" bass, magnified by the water. Birds tweeting in the bushes would serenade our exploration, as three high school boys stood up precariously peering in all directions. At times we would even stand on the seats! And why we never fell in is a testament to youth.

West Twin Lake is beautiful, and we tried to learn as much as we could about it. We learned that to the north, there was a settlement of people years ago who lived on one side of one of those mountains. We knew that there was limestone in the area, and we heard that there were caves nearby. Canaan had a limestone quarry.

With further investigation (especially by my friend Warren), we discovered that, to the south of West Twin, there was a cave opening in the woods. That opening led to a cave that went *under the lake*! Now that got our attention. As we asked around, we found a "kid" who had entered that cave with a friend. I can't remember his name, but the land is posted.

He explored a bit of it, and we heard it was "tight" inside and went steeply downhill. We also heard a rumor that in the 1800's, the cave was a tourist attraction or something. The hill to the south is even called "Cave Hill" on some maps. Anyway, being off limits legally, we never pursued it further but delighted in the fact that maybe we knew something others didn't. The mysterious West Twin Lake *has a cave under it*!

As we got older, we gradually moved our interests to catching trout. Dad and Mom had had some good success trolling in the "big" lake with streamers, making them dart by pumping the line as one moved. We eventually gave it a shot and what do you know, started catching trout. This progression took a few years, but we were getting better and better.

Our first success, and Dad's too, was on a Mickey Finn streamer, and my friend Warren began to try some of his. He got real good at making them, and before long we were limiting out with Mickey Finns and our next favorite, the Gray Ghost. Shhhh – we kept it top-secret of course. Warren's brothers, Bob and John, would troll too, and sometimes my brother Hal and his friend, Steve O'Hara would be there. We had great competitions. Our favorite spot was along the road, skirting the drop-offs, and both sides of the big island.

Around this time, we also discovered a spot of land the state owned, located just before you get to O'Hara's Landing (the owners were not related to our friend Steve). There was only room for two cars, but if you were there early enough, and lucky enough, you could park and carry the boat across the road and over the guard rail, and plunk it into the lake – for free! And we did so many times.

As time went on, we got better and better. Mom and Dad also started bobber fishing, and minnows were our next find.

Dad had moved up to a better boat at this time. He got a Cruisers Inc. sixteen foot white wooden lapstrake boat. It was a honey, with a deck, windshield, and a thirty-five horsepower motor. It came with a canvas roof and curtains too.

Because East Twin was a "zoo" on opening day, my parents would launch on Friday evening and anchor in the lake. They would close the canvas flaps and sleep in the boat, being all ready for opening day at six the next morning. And you wonder where I get my excitement from!

We young folks began to anchor up here and there and minnow fish, too, if trolling didn't produce. I loved trolling, and got good at maneuvering the boat everywhere. I loved watching the barn and tree swallows, all dressed up in blue, looking like butlers with wings. They would dip and dive everywhere, eating bugs too small to see. They were there by the hundreds, and when the fishing was slow, Richie would try to trip them up behind the boat by raising his line quickly! Boys do that! The good news was he never succeeded because those birds were fast and alert.

We also discovered another bait when we began to bobber fish; perch bugs. They were called that because perch couldn't resist them. The Marina sold them sometimes, and my parents had great luck with them. And, like minnows, they caught everything.

With a little investigation, we found out perch bugs were dragonfly nymphs and they could be found on the bottom of rocks. Now, the second lake had rocks and Dad and I had caught some there. So being frugal (and sometimes broke) high school kids, we began to catch our own bait. Sometimes it took hours, splashing around the shore, running up and down railroad tracks, shoes and pants wet, catching those ugly bugs, but boy did they work. As I think back, I think we enjoyed catching bait as much as fishing. And there were so many new things to look up in the library; this kind of bug, that kind of bug, etc.

Now, bobber fishing leads to more things, like more rods! And the boat began to fill up. We gradually got to the point where we had to go to the shore and stretch a bit. And it didn't take long before we tried to get our limits in trout, bass, and pickerel all on the same day. I can't remember accomplishing it, but we came close a few times. I suppose if you count undersized fish, we did it, but that's cheating.

We kind of grew up for a few years on those two lakes, fishing in all types of weather and conditions, as nature toughened us up. We were at least smart enough to take cover during lightning episodes and we never did find rain gear that worked!

There was one time in the summer when we three decided to fish all night and with parents permission we headed out. We stocked up on some food which we kept in the car and had a great time doing our thing the first day. When we began to sag a little, we had hot dogs or hamburgers at the marina, and hit the car in the evening for more supplies.

We then went to the second lake, West Twin, for twilight and darkness. We got real silly, and had laughing and joking episodes in the darkness. We tanked up on Coke and Fudgetown cookies, and kind of lost a little composure due to lack of sleep or tiredness. At one point we couldn't stop laughing, and we thought we were getting drunk – on Coke and cookies! Eventually we went to shore on a spit of land near the railroad tracks, and tried to lie down and catch some ZZZ's in the bushes and grass. No luck – the mosquitoes owned that turf!

We fished the rest of the night, trolling Jitterbug's and Crazy Crawlers and whatnot, till daylight came. And Fudgetown cookies became an integral part of our future trips.

It was probably about this time in our "development" that we discovered heartburn! One could hear, "Wow, man, give me some water!". Anyway, it's really interesting how much junk food a twelve foot boat can hold. Yes, we ate Ma's sandwiches, but the main stuff was the cookies, candy bars, and chips we all shared. The fruit would often go last! Anyway, very soon, Rolaids became a staple in our coolers!

I don't know how, but we made it home safely (good ol' youth) and never fished all night again. It's not quite what it is cracked up to be and I never did get around to trying night salmon fishing by lantern, but I hear its fun.

We enjoyed many hours of talking and trolling on those lakes, and found favorite spots that I still fish to this day.

There is one small footnote to this trolling that perhaps only I can appreciate. See if you enjoy it too. Many times during these trips, there were lulls in the action. I, as "motor runner", always remained more or less alert. Some opening days were like crowded freeways! But more often than not, whoever was up front trolling, be it Warren, Steve, or Richie, would doze off to the hum of the engine. I would watch as the eyes would get heavier and heavier, and their pole would begin to rest on the gunwale.

Perhaps it wasn't nice, but as Flip Wilson would say, "The devil made me do it". I would turn the boat a little so I could grab my buddy's line, and, yes, give it a good quick yank! Ever do that? Boy did that get action! You never saw anyone come to attention faster. And as hard as I would try, I couldn't keep a straight face. Eventually I had to stop in order to stay alive! But I would later use the technique on my own kids, until that, too, "wasn't funny Dad"!

Sometime in my late teens, during my young and foolish years, I went ice fishing at Twin, too. I went alone, not good, and took a sled. I embarked from East Twin (O'Hara's Landing) and was determined to go to West Twin – a walk indeed.

The weather was threatening, overcast and gray, with little wind. There was hardly any snow on the ice. The lake had four or five inches of ice, and I made the trek over the causeway on the northwest corner of the island, then went down the lake, past the "Castle", and over a spit of land to the second lake. I may have caught a few pickerel or perch, nothing impressive that I remember, but weather closed in and it began to rain.

Eventually, I left West Twin for home, and had to cross East Twin again. This time I chose a shorter route, right across the middle, steering to the right around the big Island. Well, things got "hairy and scary". The ice had begun to separate from the steady, hard rain. And cracks, five or six inches across, began to form in the middle of the lake. Water was everywhere. I jumped the cracks, here, there, everywhere in my path, and pulled my sled over them as the rain poured down! I got pretty scared since no one was out there and wet dark ice really looks thin. "Would I make it across before it melted?" went through my mind.

A bit of praying took place, as I carefully maneuvered and jumped my way toward my far-off destination. I thought I would never get back to the car.

I learned a few lessons that day. First was, don't be stupid again. I have, many times since, worn a life jacket when ice fishing, especially when alone. And ice testing is a must! Anything questionable, don't go. I have even worn a long rope tethered near shore for safety. And now I usually follow the same route home that I take going out.

As the years rolled on, Twin Lakes would get visited from time to time, summer and winter, its beauty tucked peacefully away in the hills of Connecticut's northwest. And I guess we all learn lessons. The trick is to learn them without getting "creamed" in the process. I'm always amazed at how many of us manage to grow up and escape harm.

Chuckle 12

When trolling for trout, why does someone cross in front of you just as you're approaching the good spot?

O'Hara's Landing, Twin Lakes, Salisbury, CT.

Chapter 13

We Discover Lakeville
(Wononskopomuc)

Toward the end of the "Twin Lakes era", we discovered the balsam floating minnow. That lure became a permanent part of our tackle boxes, and became a primary lure.

I think our first ones were bought at Myrtle Mills, in Unionville, Ct. and were nondescript off-brand models. They were gold, about five inches long or so, and floated nicely when cast. A few tiny twitches and pauses, and wham, bass on! Pickerel loved them, too. It didn't take long for us to prefer the Rapala brand over the Rebel brand, and we quickly became experts with their use. We had good luck trolling the small ones for trout, and found that they worked in the Farmington River, too.

Warren's father, Wilbur, was a lifetime fisherman too and eventually coaxed us to give Lake Wononskopomuc in Lakeville, Ct. a try. Dad's boat had a big motor, so he never launched at Lakeville, since it had a 9.9 horsepower limit. We set out to explore the place.

We had great expectations and were shortly introduced to wooden boats you could rent. They had a fish storage area under the middle seat. If you lifted up two parts of the seat, there were holes in the bottom of the boat and water under the seat where you could store fish to keep them alive. What an idea! The boat was like a barge, but it was bigger than mine and the wind didn't blow it around as much. Sometimes the waves would lap over the sides as we came in with a heavy west wind, and one would have to be very careful. At times we would use my boat, but other times we would chip in and rent one. More often than not, we would have to bail the thing out, especially if it had rained the night before. They also tended to leak some during the day. No problem though, they provided bail cans and young kids don't mind wet feet.

That lake had fish, too. When using the restroom, one could not miss seeing the pictures on the wall of big trout and bass that had been caught there. It even had the state record for lake trout, still standing today.

We always looked forward to checking the bulletin board pictures in the office before we went out on the lake. The office guys and gals would always tell us what was hitting or not.

In later years, I made the acquaintance of a pleasant fellow, a Mr. Romeo, and he was so nice to let us know the latest fishing scuttlebutt.

If we had extra cash, we'd buy minnows swimming in the old Coke machine. We'd buy a few candy bars (I liked Baby Ruth's) on the way out and maybe one before we drove home. Unlike the great hot dogs we got at Twin Lakes, there was no hot food at Lakeville.

No matter, the fishing was hot enough. We began to catch trout, nice trout and landed and lost some big ones. But we really concentrated on bass while most others were after trout. The Rapalas worked very well and we started using the sinking ones too. They produced results, both in the gold and the silver pattern, and some days they worked wonders.

There is a great shallow area off the picnic grove and we found bass there, and bigger ones off the edges. Some went four to six pounds. I tended to like the deeper water, but my buddies of course liked the shallows. There were hundreds of "polite" compromises, but we often picked up huge bass in the shallows early in the day. Both Warren and his brother Bob became real adept at coaxing five pound-plus bass from their lairs and I got my share, too. We liked the shorelines to the west of the boat launch, and often took half-a-day to cast to almost every area along shore. Casting away from shore often worked too, if one was patient.

When we anchored for trout in one of our favorite secret spots, we were rarely disappointed. Warren was really good at it, and we became prolific bobber and minnow fishermen. Warren experimented with different pound tests, and we became convinced that four pound test line should become top secret! We often limited out rather quickly.

Before we abandon Twin Lakes for Lakeville, we had discovered another dynamite technique- trolling minnows. Now there was an art to this. One could buy this little rig thing that came with a needle. I think Mr. Aivaz, the minnow guy, put us onto it. With the needle, one could string a minnow on the rig. If the minnow was attached correctly, so it wouldn't spin, the spring trout, and sometimes a trophy, would absolutely nail that rig! If the minnow spun, one was destined for tangle trouble, and not many fish. With this rig and a few split shot, all three of us would sometimes limit out in no time.

Well, the rig worked at Lakeville too. It wasn't long before we were rigging it behind Warren's homemade spinners and "cowbells", pulling lines of blades through the water. Warren made them with the Herter's stuff he ordered. We even took salmon in both lakes this way. I still use those minnow rigs today, but have modified them with bigger double hooks.

Around this time, we discovered something that I covet to this day. It was the "blue book". Named a <u>Fishery Survey of the Lakes and Ponds of Connecticut,</u> it contained write-ups and depth maps of most of the lakes in Connecticut, and its' cover was blue. This was a jewel that complimented our geological maps, since it showed bottom details, drop-offs, and humps that exist under water. We studied the book relentlessly, like it was fish catechism!

"Where are the drop-offs?"

"That can't be right."

"I didn't know it was that deep (or shallow) there."

"Didn't we catch some there?"

Plans, plans, plans, we made plans.

That book's pages were copied more times than I can count, and we put little red X's in the secret spots to try. Over the years, people were so nice to me that now I have three copies of that prized book.

I don't think there ever was another survey done of all the Connecticut lakes, and most new books are reprints of the old depth maps. That survey was printed in 1959, and is still useful today.

Using the book, we progressed and experimented. My collection of offbeat, "why did I buy that" lures, increased, and eventually we had more than one tackle box. Rapalas occupied one by themselves. I am at the age now where, sometime soon, I'll have to liquidate some of those "no good" beauties. But they're so beautiful! They *should* work, and some did. They might even work again! Maybe I'll hold them for my grandkids. They'd look great on a wall or maybe in a shadow box; but my wife doesn't think so. And the cellar is already full of other junk (motors, poles, nets, etc.). Oh well, I'll put it off for now.

One lure that really hit for us back then was the Flatfish, only not the small one this time. Wononskopomuc had big fish, and some lived rather deep. The maps showed steep drop-offs, and we needed something that would go down there. It would be years till I mastered jigs but we got bold and bought big Flatfish lures.

The Flatfish lure on a long cast downwind would dig deep. If one used a two-handed cast carefully, the lure wouldn't tangle. We'd stop it just before it hit the water. After on and off attempts, the lure started hitting. We tried the U20 size, and then moved up to the big boy, the M2 size. I always thought "M" meant Muskie. Anyway, the M2 frog pattern became the find of the century for us. It went fifteen to twenty feet deep. Eventually the perch and natural scale patterns started to work too, and we sent away for these beauties and casted our arms off. They cost some money, so we went to seventeen pound test line, and often retied.

We caught some big bass, but one had to stick with it to do it. Sometimes we would get only one or two big four to six pound bass a day, but it was always worth the effort. We found out that some of the lures would go deeper than others, same model, same color! The deeper ones were best. So guess which ones got traded? It also gave us an excuse to order a few more, too.

We found that the end of May and the beginning of June were about the best times for big bass. The weeds aren't as thick, and that time of year is beautiful, of course.

To this day, I still have a collection of Flatfish, in another tackle box, but I don't seem to have the arm to throw them all day. They don't make some of these patterns anymore, so maybe that's a good excuse to just admire them in the box.

I still have several certificates and pins from the state for trophy fish. Some of the thanks go to those lures and techniques. If you're ever on Lakeville, you may see me making a few casts with those things, flying over my boat downwind. And these days I take a picture, and release all big fish so they can fight again another day.

Chuckle 13

Ever wonder if you put the oil in the gas for the outboard? Then you add more and smoke up everything!!

Wononskopomuc boat docks-1983

Chapter 14

Other Lakes, Too:
More Wheels

Over the years, Lake Wononskopomuc really became one of our favorite destinations. However, as high school kids think, there are always greener pastures. We often didn't have the funds to go fifty miles to fish, so we took a shot at other lakes and places closer to home.

Richie had a cousin who lived on Ledge Road in Plainville, and he tipped us off to a lake just up from him called the Plainville Reservoir. We investigated, and were promptly told we needed a permit to get into the reservoir. Further fact-finding revealed that five permits per week were issued to town residents who might want to fish the place. We got permits, and fish we did.

Dreams of big fish and the rumors of such soon faded when we could only catch small, over abundant perch and sunnies. The lake was hard to maneuver around, with bushes, rocks, snakes, and poison ivy all over the place. But we fished anyway, especially in the fall, when the leaves were down and we discovered some nice brown bullheads. They became the prize and we had some good times.

One summer we decided to really try bullhead fishing at night there. Now, on this occasion, we did not have permission and night fishing was not allowed. I remember "the three musketeers" sneaking in at dusk on the south side of the lake.

We went about halfway down the lake for about fifteen or twenty minutes, and found some nice, flat, big rectangular rocks to sit on, and started bullhead fishing. Talk, fish, talk, fish, shhhh, etc. – be quiet – watch the light! We had a ball, doing whatever kids do, and tried not to tangle in the darkness and we got some catfish, too. We put them on a stick and swatted mosquitoes. Somewhere around midnight or so, we made our way back out, muddy shoes, scratched arms and all. The burdock that was stuck in our clothes was a pain but we jumped in the car and headed home, another fond adventure achieved.

In previous years, when I was just a youngster, my parents didn't just take us on rides for ice cream, or rides to see the Christmas lights at night – Dad took me ice fishing too. One place he heard of was Lake Lillinonah, which was supposed to have big perch. We made our way to a dirt road and down some hills that gave us access to the Shepaug branch of the lake. My memory is hazy, but a few things have stuck in my memory. One was that we had an ice spud (chopper) and the second was that the ice seemed three feet thick. I also remember that I was the hole chopper and that spud didn't seem too sharp! We set up our tip-ups and I was fascinated (and pooped!). I guess I became an ice fisherman from that day forward. We caught a few fish that day and I still have Dad's intriguing tip-ups.

This trip taught me some of the beauty of the winter sport, and the second trip taught me caution! Dad and I went to a snow-covered Bantam Lake, unpacked, and started out on the lake. Dad made me trail him, for safety reasons. It wasn't long before he yelled, "Get back, get back!" He had fallen through a layer of ice that was under the snow, and dropped into several inches of water, and then stopped. On his second step he did the same thing, and he turned, motioned me to shore, and tried to scramble in my direction too.

We got to shore a-ok, but Dad sort of got the snot scared out of him. And as a wide-eyed boy, I was pretty shook up, too! Apparently, water had been trapped between two layers of ice, and one had no idea how thick layer number two was, especially with the snow on top. We went home!

When I go out now, I always use test holes if there is any doubt whatsoever! Good lesson learned and thankfully, we both survived.

During the high school years, Warren, Richie, and I ice fished the reservoir periodically. I used the skills Dad had taught me. The perch were a bit undersized, but one could take a bucket load home and tip-up action would become fast and furious. "Flag! Flag!" was heard often. What a sweet refrain.

Bait would often run out, and we learned rather quickly that perch eyes worked as well as live bait. We also started using lures to ice fish, and this reservoir gave up a lot of fish to the jigging gold or silver Rapala, the little small skinny one. That was another secret we tried to keep. We even tried crazy things like putting crushed egg shells down the hole to act like glitter attractant. It didn't work and I won't even tell you what other "attractants" we made in the blender, but they didn't work either. On the coldest of days the fish would quickly freeze solid. When things slowed down we'd carve a little reservoir in the ice to keep the fish alive. Sometimes we would get a little hockey going with the ice chunks. Other times we would play three-man perch football. And the football, yup, a frozen perch, worked very well!

During these years, my parents were nice enough to trust me with the family car, and even though most "dates" were with lakes, a girl date here and there began to interfere with progress. And if anything will get in the way of progress that will! And it did, more and more.

I also began to apply to colleges, as did most of my friends. I still worked for the Minors and began to paint, paper, and do general handyman work. They realized that I would probably need a car when I decided to go to CCSC in New Britain. I was going to become a teacher, and was going to commute to college.

And bless them for they allowed me to buy a car from them for fifty "whole" dollars! The car was a four-door, straight eight, four speed automatic, a 1946 gray Oldsmobile. It was a honey. The backseat looked like a sofa and the car was heavy. Now I had my own wheels. The hood was so big; you couldn't even see the right fender. No problem. And did I have a ball in that car. I washed and waxed it to death, too!

We burned some gas up cruising Bristol McDonalds, the three of us too timid to meet anybody. I did most of the driving, since I get car sick if I ride.

We played a lot of sandlot basketball, and some touch football during those times too. We had a "snow bowl" game every year for a while. Marathon lure bargaining continued and more fishing areas close to home became explored.

A place we heard of in those years drew us east toward Kensington, CT. We discovered the Hart Ponds, full of weeds and "big" bass. If one could get the lure between the weed pads, some big bass would hit.

Perhaps our most memorable outing there took place ice fishing, too. We figured that we could set up between and amongst the weedy areas. There was a snowstorm due the day we planned to fish but being young and stupid, we only saw that as a challenge. Getting there was no problem. We went out on the lake, set up, and had our usual fun, but caught little. It snowed all day. I've done this several times, fished in the snow, and have never had much luck that I can remember. It is nasty and a pain to keep the holes open but then it was young fun!

Who cares, we were "pioneers" – Davy Crockett types (I had one of those hats when I was younger!). Our only problem occurred when we tried to go home. The dirt road was relatively unused, with ruts galore, and it became hard to maneuver. I got up a head of steam with that old car and went plowing through. The straight eight '46 Oldsmobile was heavy and tank- like, but the snow was deep. I stopped the car when I heard a strange sound. We got out, and discovered the gas tank had been pulled off and it was sitting on the ground under the car.

Somehow we jacked the thing up, lay in the snow, and pushed the gas tank back in place, with the metal bands again underneath it. It was still snowing hard, but we somehow careened out of there, the ol' car none the worse for wear. And I never did touch it again! That ol' car was nicked named "The Grey Goose", and it sure "flew" us home that day. We were crazy kids living by our wits.

I had another incident with that beloved first car of mine, that hydromatic monster. I don't know if it was Warren or a friend named Jimmy Davis that was with me, but we decided to ice fish East Twin Lake. Freezing rain was predicted in the morning? So what!

We went up route 44, through Collinsville, to New Hartford, through Winsted with no problem. As we approached Norfolk, the road began to get dicey. Freezing rain had developed, and I slowed a bit. But as it turned out, I didn't slow enough! I came around a corner where there is a sweeping curve with a gas station and a pond on the right. Cars were in the ditch on both sides of the road and traffic was stopped for an accident. A policeman was running toward me, with great motions to slow down, stop. I couldn't and I wasn't going that fast! But Dad taught me a bit about using brakes on ice. I pumped my brains out as the officer, just in time, jumped over the guard rail to safety. I couldn't stop! A car in front was looming, as I gently pulled left – oh, oh – car coming head-on – pulled right into another spot, and then left again, and I dodged at least eight cars on alternate sides, finding openings in survival mode! We finally stopped on the shoulder past the whole mess, absolutely astounded we missed everyone. Some cars weren't so lucky. The officer finally came to us, and to our surprise, said we did a great job, and we could continue. We waited for the sand truck!

I have no idea if we caught anything that day, but we never turned back. We must have had angels on our roof as we were guided through what could've been a demolition derby or worse. Or maybe it was the officer that had the angel. Anyway, thanks for angels!

Chuckle 14

Why is the car the farthest away when you discover you launched the boat with the plug out!

Chapter 15

Vacations

I mentioned before that my family vacationed at Fair Haven Beach State Park, in New York, when I was quite young. My grandfather and grandmother were of a rare breed of folks back then that towed a small house trailer. Gramps was probably one of the last of a "breed" of Singer sewing machine repair men that serviced specific routes, both up north, and, in the winter, down south. He would work his way through New England, upstate New York, and all the way to Michigan, stopping along the way to service people's sewing machines. In the fall, he would work his way back south. When we visited Fair Haven, he was there at a private trailer camp. He and Dad would fish and they would cast and cast (L&S Mirror Lures mostly) for "white bass". The bass would run in schools and sometimes the action was great. Gramps loved fishing and was good at it.

Well, in addition to the Fair Haven visits, I remember our family getting excited about visiting Dad's father and mother at another New York location. I learned they were at a place called Selkirk Shores State Park in Pulaski, New York. Now little kids pick up excitement like magnets pick up nails and we were all excited about going there.

But I had a problem. I started feeling a little sick the day before leaving but said nothing. I did not want to mess up the trip. Anyway, with my neck stiff, my brother and I piled into the back seat (we sat on the arm rests), and we were off. About halfway there, my mother started to get clued in that something wasn't right; mothers are like that!

"Look at me," she said. "Look at me!"

I did. After the initial gasp, came "Oh my God, he's got the mumps!"

I would experience that gasp again, years later (poor Mom). When I was about twelve she picked us kids up at Norton Park after playing baseball. Riding home, I sat quietly on the back seat. She looked into the rear view mirror and insisted I had been eating chocolate because of the residue on my face. After shaking my head no twice, I smiled at her. Both of my permanent front teeth had been knocked out when I "smiled at a fastball"! Luckily, we didn't hit a tree!

Anyway, it was too late to turn back now. I had accomplished my mission. Mom and Dad pitched the army tent and cots next to Gramp's trailer, and the site turned into a "MASH" unit! We were kept in the tent – yep, my brother Hal got mumps too – and in the dim light for I don't know how long. Everyone was afraid we would get kicked out of the campground and I couldn't go fishing with Gramps and Dad. Eventually we played in the grass, with our cars and sticks, and Mom and Gram took us to the playground as we got better. Through a child's eyes, there seemed to be some pretty big cliffs there, too. At least we had a vacation that I never forgot.

As the years went by, Dad learned of a great campsite in the Adirondacks from a camper at Fair Haven. Eventually we started going there, and we never looked back. At this campground we could camp right on the water. Named Fish Creek Ponds Public Campground, we found that we could even build our own dock and one could boat from lake to lake. The campground was located on a clover leaf of four lakes. They were fed by Fish Creek itself. To me it was a fisherman's paradise, and my circle expanded with my age. I went, at eleven years old, from fishing from a dock, to fishing from a boat, to trying different lakes as I became older. I eventually ended up on many Adirondack lakes as an adult. If I were to write a second book, it would be about this place, its beauty and the profound effect it has had on me over my last fifty seven years of visits.

Our family would sometimes also run up north in the fall or spring for a three-day holiday. As kids, sometimes we were allowed to bring our friends, and Richie Roman came with us on one such occasion.

Richie and I were there to fish! And the mountains can get wet. No problem – we had ponchos. Anyway, we rowed to the creek, about a half-mile, and rowed about a mile up the creek to a pond called Copperas Pond. We fished in the drizzle along the way, mostly for bass. When we got to Copperas, the water was clear to light bluish. It was a very pristine place. We fished the east bay and then decided to troll down the south side of the small pond. Richie put on about a three and a half inch gold "mongrel" lure, threw it out, and we rowed. I forgot what I used, probably a bass lure.

Well, we went for about fifty yards and wham! – Richie had a fish on. It dove, it jumped – what the heck – it was a northern pike! We always wished we could catch one but never did. We never thought we could catch pike. It was our first pike! It ran a few times and we finally netted it. Not that big, but a "monster" to us at that time.

If one watched us from shore, it must have looked like two hobos' doing a "dance of the fish". We were whooping and hollering. We stringered the fish, and in spite of many attempts, caught nothing else that day.

Mom cooked it up for us, and nothing was ever sweeter! That fish started me on a trek, a journey for years to come, to track down northern pike on vacations. We had a few in Connecticut, but those up North captured years of my attention!

Do you know it took two to three years for me to get Richie to trade that lure to me! And I paid a hefty price in lures. And once I had the lure, I didn't use it because I didn't want to lose it. Stupid, huh! I still have the lure.

When we were in high school we brought Warren up to the mountains too. I was relentless on my quest for fish on our summer vacations. Once, Warren and I snuck out to fish at night, and we trolled Jitterbugs on Follensby Pond. We had a few hits, but learned how dark it really is when there is a new moon. New moon – what moon – no moon! Very dark! Lesson learned.

We loved waterskiing in the heat of the day. Dad's boat could tow skiers and the whole family learned how to ski. There were times when Dad got pretty tired of towing us.

One day, we decided to teach Warren how to ski. You need to know two things about Warren. One, he was a determined individual (translates to stubborn), and two, he had poor vision without his thick glasses. Anyway, we started teaching Warren. First, the signals; a big circle with our arms meant once more around. Pointing in means we're going in, and, in Warren's case, waving a big towel means "let go"(i.e. he couldn't see).

He tried to get up, several times, with us all yelling "arms straight, knees bent." No luck. But Hal, my brother, and I had mastered the art of skiing right off the end of the dock by just stepping onto the skis as the rope tightened. We showed him, and he liked that idea. It seemed easier than plowing him all over the lake.

The water was about three or four feet deep at the end of the homemade dock. We got him all set. Dad idled out. "Arms straight knees bent!"

"Hit it Dad!" was the call. Now Warren was a bit more muscular and a bit heavier than us. Off he went, right to the bottom! Where was he? Let go! Oh, oh, we forgot to tell him to let go!

That stubborn fellow must have gone thirty or forty feet underwater along the bottom, bumping everything, before popping out behind the boat like a cruise missile. And everything was intact, and he was still holding position! He was skiing, seaweed and all. I told you he was determined!

We had many happy hours after that, but that bottom bumping ski story has been told over and over around the campfire. No one has ever seen anyone go that far underwater.

That "Richie" northern pike launched me on a quest that entertained me for years. I returned to that lake many times, both with my kayak and my twelve foot boat. I read a lot of articles and collected many lures. Dad learned, and then showed me, how to string a hook through the back of a sucker chub bait, and fish near the weeds with giant three inch bobbers. We would wait, and when the bobber went down, we wouldn't pull. We waited for it to come up. When it went down a second time, then we would pull, and fight! Wow, what great fun.

But big bait wasn't always available and was expensive. Once I had a boat and motor, I was off and trolling. I put hours and hours on that little five horsepower Johnson. Once I got on vacation, I trolled almost every morning and evening for two or three week's straight, depending on the length of our vacation. My parents must have had peaceful times, restful for them. I just trolled my brains out!

I got to know every weed bed and hole in many of the accessible lakes. I found that if one trolled a Daredevil and/or a Redeye Wiggler (I had all three – copper, gold, silver), one could catch some real nice northerns. I had to just miss the weeds and I got real good at trolling.

I trolled in the rain; I trolled in the sun. I trolled in the fog, in the heat, and in the cold. Maybe I really was Daniel Boone!

At one time I trolled past an island and the Girl Scouts were camped there. Three ran out on a dock and waved. I was always quite shy, but I smiled, waved back, and kept on moving. But it kind of made my day, if you know what I mean. I tried to look manly!

On one of those times when Warren and I went out, we navigated through almost blinding fog. We gently made our way through Spider Creek to Follensby Clear Pond. Warren wondered how I was able to find my way. I was gaining experience.

In a few minutes we heard a motor and came across three guys in a boat. They flagged us down and asked directions. They explained that they were lost and had been looking for the stream to get out of there and had been following the shore "for miles". Barely able to contain myself, I pointed them toward where we had come from, and they motored off that way. Warren asked, "Why are you busting at the seams?"

Barely containing myself, I explained to Warren that the guys were following the shoreline, hardly visible through the fog, for hours and getting nowhere. They were going around and around an island! In the fog, everything looks the same and I guess it was good we came along. I never forgot that.

A few years before, when I was alone, I got my biggest northern in that lake. I was trolling at about 6 AM and it was raining. I had my casting pole set up with a big Daredevil and was trolling through a place called "the Narrows". My pole bent over and as I pulled, nothing moved. I killed the motor and got ready to push the boat backward thinking that I had hooked a log. Ker-splash – nope, not a log– a big fish jumped high and the fight was on. That fish ran and lunged time after time and I thought I would never land it. Smartly, I carried a big net, and slid it under the fish and scooped it up with two hands, throwing the pole aside. Did that fish thrash! I covered it with my body till it calmed down. I did not let it jump out of the boat and I was one happy, happy guy!

I eventually slid the fish under the seat so it wouldn't jump out, and covered it with wet rags. I secured him with three or four stringer hooks to make sure he wouldn't get away and then tried to clean the slime that was all over the place. It was still early and raining. But it was sun-shining in my brain! I was warm as toast. Nothing warms one up like catching a big fish.

I couldn't go proudly back to camp yet – no one was up. It was hard, but I continued to half heartedly fish till about 8 AM – till I couldn't stand it anymore, and then headed back to camp. The bragging rights were all mine that day. The fish was about twelve pounds and over thirty-eight inches long. I never caught a northern that big ever again and I was just a high school kid at the time.

Some places and some lakes provide special "chapels" in one's heart. Follensby Clear Pond is one of those places. A year or two later, my friend Warren and I were on the lake one morning, once again making our way through fog, searching for pike. Warren was casting while I slowly trolled toward a destination. We were out in the middle of the lake somewhere when the fog began to swirl a bit and a hole opened above us in the sky. The sun started shining through and suddenly, like bright lights, the fog lit up with color! We were seeing every blue, yellow, and pink color imaginable, our boat surrounded by a giant circular moving wall, blue sky above. We had our own private beam of sunshine. I have never seen anything like it since in my life – kind of a taste of heaven! So startled by the spectacular scene around us, we both put down our poles, and sat, observing the incredible jaw-dropping event around us. I was speechless and awed! As quickly as it was created, it dispersed. We both felt that we went to church that day in the boat. A message, a signal, an omen – certainly something *special* shared with a dear friend – happened that day.

I have visited that lake countless times through the years since, and never tire of its beauty and serenity.

Quiet episodes on lakes give us strength and renewal, and revitalize the "kid" in us. They have an addictive quality, a positive pull that makes our sport quite unique. Each time out we grow a little. It keeps fishermen young, and mellow, too; young enough to want to go out again sometime, no matter your age. Lakes seem to always be beckoning to me. Even when I watch TV and see water, I seem to analyze coves and bays that might hold possibilities; habit I guess.

I am very grateful for our family vacations. Dad and Mom not only taught us how to work, but taught us priorities. No matter what, we went on vacation and some of my fondest memories were born and nurtured there.

It still takes me weeks to get ready for vacation, but I find fun in the planning and anticipation. And learning how to fish became learning how to plan.

Chuckle 15

There must be a way to get the fish smell out of rain gear stored in the five gallon fish bucket!

My big Northern Pike

Chapter 16

Twin Lakes & the Hogback

Earlier I mentioned that a fellow named Joe Aivaz sold bait in town. He was a policeman, and loved to trout fish. I was active at the time in my Methodist church, and had many interactions with Rev. Jim Davis. Rev. Jim and Joe would fish several times in the spring, and they invited me to go once, too. I jumped at the chance, and off we went to Rogers Lake. Joe had a favorite spot in the northwestern area of the lake where he would limit out quickly. That's all I can reveal. We had great luck that day, too.

Sometimes fishing friends can cause one to do "extraordinary" things. Some people use the word "foolhardy", but I prefer "extraordinary"! I was in my late teens when Rev. Davis and his family went on vacation somewhere in New York. On the way home, they got into a terrible accident on the New York Thruway, and their family ended up in intensive care at the Albany Medical Center. The whole congregation prayed for their recovery, and they made slow but positive progress over the next few weeks.

I wanted to visit, but the hospital informed people that only immediate family and clergy were allowed as they recuperated. And so it was that I became "clergy". I took a white shirt and put it on backwards, then put another black pullover shirt over it. I now had a collar like ministers wear! A suit jacket and a Bible to hold made the rest of the outfit. My buddy Richie went with me, and when we got to the Albany Medical Center, I had Richie wait in the lobby, and pretend he didn't know me, in case I got into trouble.

I got the room number, and holding my Bible in my left hand against my chest, I got into the elevator. From a few people I got "Good morning Father" and responded with, "Good morning, God bless you" as I tried to stay as non-descript as possible.

I got off on the appropriate floor, and after saying "Bless you" a few times found Davis's room. As I walked in I saw he had company, and Rev. Jim greeted me with surprise!

"How long was I unconscious?" he gasped, as he noticed my "clergy" collar! His company happened to be one of the higher-up bishops of the church. He looked me over, smiled, and then excused himself and walked out.

As I explained to my pastor that I just had to see him for a minute to wish him well, he was delighted with my "disguise" and insisted on taking me to see his recovering wife Bjorg. She too got a kick out of my visit, and after some small talk, I made my way out.

I picked up Richie with a nod of the head, and we went to the car. I stopped to pay the parking fee on the way out and got the frosting on the cake! There was no charge, the man said, Clergy park free and home with satisfaction I went. As I think back, I am sure the Bishop knew something was up. A backwards white shirt doesn't quite make a clergy collar. But fishing creates bonds among people that seem to become lifetime gems.

The college years kept me quite busy and my part-time work helped pay some of the bills. In addition to lawn mowing and weeding, I began to paint and did handyman work for the Minors. I learned to wallpaper, and enjoyed being Mr. Fix-it when things needed repairs.

From the early years on up I became quite mechanical too, ever since Dad had me "hold the flashlight" while fixing the car. We also installed TV antennas on roofs when I was younger. We put up conical antennas and UHF – VHF stuff. While I held the masts, Dad would screw in the bolts for the guy wires, but first we had to find the best spot on the roof for reception. As I think back, I think they stole our act for "Married with Children" episodes, but we didn't fall! Our last job was on a slate roof, three stories up, with me tied to the chimney with a safety rope. That was Dad's last antenna job – too scary!

We also worked some on outboards too. For some reason, Dad's motor often broke down on vacation! Maybe we skied too much.

Anyway, I painted outside in the summers and even did some roofing work. Many rooms were redone in the winter months also but I was never too busy to fish. As a matter-of-fact, during some college semesters, I arranged my courses so that I had to go on Mondays, Wednesdays, and Fridays and had very light loads on Tuesdays and

Thursdays. I remember being quite proud of myself, sitting in my twelve foot Starcraft boat, somewhere in West Twin Lake. I was anchored, glancing at bobbers in the sunshine, and had my books open on the middle seat. Yes, I was studying and doing homework out on the lake. Now that's making good use of one's time! I didn't do it often, but always thought it was a great way to multitask!

I didn't see Richie and Warren as much now, since they, too, had gone off to college. Sometimes I would fish with Steve O'Hara, a friend of my brother Hal's, and other times I would go alone. And a great place to fish alone was the Hogback Reservoir in the New Hartford and Colebrook area.

I would often grab a bucket of minnows and head out there. At that time one had to cross the lower dam, and walk to any good-looking spot on the shore to fish. Trout fishing was fair and the scenery and surroundings were pristine and outstanding. It wasn't long before I figured out that one could put a little boat on that lake.

Back then it wasn't easy and there really was no launch. After sliding the boat off the bars on the top of the car, I had to drag it across an expanse of grass, then down a steep bank of boulders and pull it through brambles and bushes to the water's edge. Then I had to lug the five horsepower motor, gas can, and tackle down, too and I did, with great happy effort.

I began to troll that lake and really enjoyed exploring it. There were some good holes and pockets of fish near the upper dam, and I often limited out there with minnows and bobbers. The dam protected me from the wind. I also took my share of trout on pink, silver, or green Mooseluk Wobblers trolled with downriggers.

Warren was in college at Valparaiso, Indiana and had access to some nice tackle outlets near Chicago. He was so thoughtful and sent me a small fish finder that just showed the depth and little black dots for fish. It was simple but effective, and I delighted in trolling and watching that screen. That was around 1963, and I haven't stopped using a depth finder since. What a tool! I became quite adept at using downriggers now, and had two nice small Big Jon portables. I used two Browning downrigger poles, thanks to the Fall Mountain Sports store and their great inventory! I really enjoyed their knowledgeable tips and great store.

Anyway, getting the boat out of the Hogback was no easy task; it was uphill! I used patience. I would pick the boat up by one end and walk it in a half circle, and drop it. Then I would do the same with the other end. Eventually the boat got up the bank to the car and was pulled up on the roof. What doesn't kill you makes you stronger, I guess! That lake was worth it, and I was able to observe hawks, foxes, turkeys, and even a bobcat over the years.

On one trip there it was cold as heck! It was late November, and a light snow was falling as I launched the boat. I trolled across the lake and then to the upper dam. It was so cold and snowy that I decided to turn the motor off and row to keep warm. The boat was covered in snow. As I left the upper dam I continued down the west drop-off side, sitting in snow and gently pulling on the oars. The silence and solitude wrapped around me and gave me a very enjoyable and memorable feeling.

Then, wham, a downrigger pole snapped up and I had a fish, a nice fish! I played it out and netted it in that eerie silence. A beautiful dark-colored brown, about seven pounds, ended up on my stringer. And now I was warm as I rowed back to the dam, turned around, and trolled two Mooseluks again through the same area, patiently trolling just the right distance from shore. Bang, another fish! This brown went about three and a half pounds, a nice catch. A secret here – the Mooseluks were colored in the green frog pattern-shhhh!

I tried a few more times, but it was so snowy and wet, I headed back to the lower dam and the launch. It was time to go home. I unloaded my poles and "junk" from the boat and put the fish in a big Rubbermaid tub and then tried to pull the boat out.

That became a chore! The boat was heavy! On inspection, I found out that snow and ice had built up on the outside walls of the boat. There was about an inch of ice between the gunwales and the water, all along the outside of the boat! I had to get a screwdriver and use it as a hammer to knock the ice off the boat and that took awhile. It was heavy enough without the ice! There is a gate at the Hogback and the caretaker had to wait some time for me to get that boat on my car before he could lock up for the evening. He was a patient and kind fellow, and I finally left with my two nice trout. A nice day indeed!

I spent many fine days on that lake, and even ended up there, fishing from shore with minnows while I listened to the radio broadcast the funeral of John Kennedy. College had been canceled that day, and by myself at a lake is where I wanted to be as I contemplated what had happened. And I was alone with my thoughts.

Chuckle 16

Ever slam the trunk of a car and shorten a fishing rod?

Hogback Brown Trout

Chapter 17

End of the College Years
(Off to Manitoba!)

Most of my time was used up just going to college, working, some dating, vacationing, and just hanging out with my friends. But fishing was threaded through much of this tapestry.

I began to get the urge to fish north, as in Canada or Alaska. Well, why not dream big. I began to read about pike and muskie fishing in far-off places where fish just "jump in the boat"! Then a place called Reed Lake, Manitoba, caught my attention. Something in those fishing magazines set it off, and I started to plan. Richie, Warren, and I talked about it a lot, and Warren was already in college at Valparaiso in Indiana. Heck, that's halfway. Even though Richie went to Clark University, plans were made to go north. Next up was the problem of money. I decided in 1964 to get a second job in order to afford this enterprise. After working afternoons for the Minors doing their gardening, I wound up opening the new McDonald's in New Britain, working nights. I worked 6 PM to midnight, and I had some 8 AM classes, too! I commuted to CSCC, but anything for the cause.

The following spring I was able to buy a 1957 Oldsmobile for $400 and we made plans for our trip to Manitoba. Richie scraped together $600 and so did I.

At the end of July, we loaded up our car with our supplies. We had that good old pup tent, sleeping bags, "tons" of cans of Dinty Moore's Beef Stew, fishing gear, and paraphernalia up the ka-zoo. McDonald's had given us about 50 free meal passes, too. The boat and the oars were tied on the roof, and the motor and gas can were in the trunk. When August 1 came, off we went.

We were disappointed when we got to Valparaiso, Indiana, because Warren had a change of plans. He was going to Ashton,

Idaho, to visit the family of the girl he just asked to marry him! Wow! One of the Three Musketeers was going to get married.

Well, there was still Richie and I, and Manitoba was still ahead. Warren gave us a bunch of plastic five gallon gas containers that he had ordered from Herter's, and we continued on our journey. We made plans to see him in Idaho.

The '57 Olds was a used car and we felt that we better baby the thing to avoid breakdowns. We decided to stay below sixty miles per hour. At one point we ended up, at night, on a road between Minneapolis and St. Paul, somehow wedged in a convoy of trucks. There seemed to be well over one hundred of them, going both ways on a two-lane road, and all wanting to do more than sixty miles per hour! With the boat on the top and white knuckles on the steering wheel, we looked like a turtle among dinosaurs. I guess we were on a main nighttime route between the two cities!

Days later we somehow ended up on the outskirts of Winnipeg, Manitoba. It was raining and warm, and the generator light was on. We pulled over, and decided to park in a parking spot right there inside the city limits. Tired, we tried sleeping in the car. It was hot and with windows opened a bit, mosquitoes ate us up. We got little sleep that night.

We got the car fixed for one dollar the next day – the generator brushes needed cleaning! And someone who liked our adventure story bought us a free breakfast at a diner. Nice! And we were on our way again

We were on our adventure, all right. Making our way north through Manitoba for many hours we finally came to a junction called Flin Flon. There was a sign pointing us toward Reed Lake. The road turned to a dirt road, hard packed with a few stones here and there. We filled the car with gas, as well as the outboard tank, and the multiple five gallon jugs sitting on the back seat. No smoking in this car!

We decided to call home and had to use an old-fashioned crank phone. We were amazed and amused when we got an operator, and asked to call Connecticut. She didn't know where Connecticut was, but looked it up in her Atlas book. Low and behold Connecticut was cut off at the end of her page!!

After the confusion we finally connected with our families and were delighted to update everyone, including the use of a crank phone. This was the last phone, so we would be out of contact for a while! We proceeded onward, one hundred and seventy-five miles on dirt roads to Reed Lake. There were places where Richie had to get out and move stones so that we wouldn't bottom out! The natives went about fifty miles an hour on those dirt roads and stones flew everywhere as they went by. But we were ready. We had placed screening on the front of the car (the fishing magazine told us to do that!) and went about half that speed.

We pitched our tent at the small Reed Lake campground consisting of six to ten sites in all. We cooked up some stew (in the can) and then went down to the campground dock. Some guy had just pulled his sputtering son out of the water! I guess he fell in – off the dock – just a little kid. We jabbered about the fishing and then someone pointed out a black cloud over the water. It was slowly approaching and someone yelled – "take cover!" We got a quick explanation. "Mosquitoes: they come this time every day! Get inside."

We ran to our tent, dove in, and zipped the screen. What a buzz! The mosquitoes were so thick that if one stood up, one wouldn't be able to see. That impressed us. In a bit, they were all gone.

We felt very tired and couldn't figure out why until we checked our watches. It was 11:30, and it was still light out. We were so far north that the sun was setting late and coming up about 4:30 A.M. since we were just south of the Arctic Circle. Off to bed we went.

The next few days we fished and fished. We caught walleyes and many northerns, some real nice. We pulled up on shore and cooked fish, just like the real guides!

One day, we went out, and it was windy. Our camp was in a bay, and as we headed out, downwind, the waves got bigger. I tried to turn out around a point and make headway up the lake, but the waves were huge. As the water came in the boat, Richie started bailing, as waves sent us up, up, up and over their tops. I couldn't turn back without swamping the boat. Waves seemed about nine feet but were probably five or better. I gently backed us up on the waves, letting them push us back toward the bay out of which we came. Richie grabbed his life jacket and held it under one arm as he bailed like crazy with the other. We thought we were goners! I kept dodging wave crests till we saw an opening to get into the sheltered bay. As we got to a place where a point of land was sheltering us a bit, I made a diagonal turn and made a run for the bay through a wave trough. We made it. The outboard never missed a beat but our hearts may have!

On another day, we headed out toward an island that was way out toward the middle. It was probably five miles out. Those Canada lakes are big but the lake was calm so we ventured out there – quite a ride. Now, I still had my old Pflueger casting reel with twenty-five pound test line, and I went for broke. I put the biggest Daredevil I think they ever made on that pole – a lure so big one could almost eat off it as a plate!

We got very apprehensive being a few miles out on that lake. We could hardly see the shore, so we started having some second thoughts. If the wind came up, we'd get stranded on rock islands, and no one knew we were out there. So we decided we'd take two or three casts – and then leave. I lobbed my lure out and cranked it in. As it came in, two huge fish, one very close to the lure, followed it toward the boat.

Now, I mean these fish were huge, humongous fish! To me they seemed five or six feet – the size of oars! Have you ever heard of buck fever? I froze. I jumped up on the middle seat and I could not turn the reel handles. The fish startled and scared me. I couldn't gasp words out fast enough to tell Richie.

That lure just fluttered to the side of the boat. I reeled it in and....left ... fish too big! I could not have held that fish with that pole and reel, even if I had hooked it. And we had no gaff (or gaff experience) either. We motored back satisfied that we had at least hooked a memory and it still lives today.

After a side trip to Snow Lake and regrettably not taking a train trip to Churchill on Hudson's Bay, we headed back south, through Saskatchewan.

We were so sick of beef stew that we were able to trade twelve cans or so for soup or something – for anything. I don't remember what we traded for, but it was better than beef stew for a change.

We crossed the border, and headed toward Warren, who was now in Ashton, Idaho. As we approached a pass in the mountains at night in the Shoshone National Forest, the generator light went on again. We drove for awhile on the "up" side of the pass, but the lights began to dim. We pulled into a little campground and pitched our pup tent. No one was around anywhere. We were the only ones in that place.

We sacked out but were soon awakened by a garbage can tumbling around. Now, I had been to the Smoky Mountains National Park with my parents, and I knew that sound. I nudged Rich, who was awake too, and asked him if he had any food in the tent. Relieved, he said no. We lay there, as a bear came to our little shelter. We could hear his feet crunch, crunch, on the pine needles as he walked. Next to the tent, his paw hit unused tent stakes that were on the ground next to me, outside. His nose must have been just above my head as I could hear him breathing in and out, in and out! I could hear his breath! And I did not breathe for an hour, I swear. Our eyes were probably the size of cereal bowls, as frozen, we stared into the black night.

The next morning (we didn't get eaten) we found big bear tracks all over our site and we figured it was a grizzly! We must have camped in his stomping ground. Anyway we got out of there and coasted down the pass to a garage. The generator was replaced and as I think back over the years, I reckon that bear knew we were in that tent.

We made our way to Yellowstone Park and camped near Old Faithful. We cooked dinner and were eating when I looked up and asked Richie not to make any sudden moves. I asked him to slowly leave the table and follow me. He did and the bear over his shoulder ate our supper!

Anyway, being young and nutty, we decided to pretend to be "rich" and entered the Yellowstone Lodge. We sat down at a table on one of the upper tiers and watched the fire below in the huge fireplace. We made out some postcards and finally left. It was nice being "wealthy" for a while.

We made our way through the park to Ashton, Idaho. There we met up again with our friend Warren and his wife-to-be, JoAnn. He was a lucky man and after visiting and seeing some great fishing spots and doing some water skiing, we left for home.

We didn't get too far before we broke down. It was later evening again as we sputtered down a hill and the car died in Moorcroft, Wyoming. We were very close to Devils Tower National Park.

We stalled almost in front of the only garage in town. The next morning they poked and fussed around with that car and said they couldn't fix it. They said the car was shot, that it had a bad engine. They offered to sell us a car for $600 but I knew that I had not blown the engine. So we finagled around and rented a bay of the garage to work on the car ourselves. They loaned us a junker and we pitched our tent out in a cow pasture.

We took that thing apart and put it back together about three times over a five-day period. Their mechanic was stumped too. The car kept firing back into the carburetor and wouldn't start. Kind of depressed and discouraged, we asked around to find another mechanic. We were sent down the street and found a retired mechanic rocking on his porch. We pleaded with him for help and he reluctantly came to the garage. With the sparkplugs out and the carburetor and intake off the engine, he asked us to turn it over using the fan blade. We were delighted when he pointed to a hydraulic lifter and said it was frozen up. We were excited and we thanked him profusely.

We tried to buy a new lifter, but had no luck. There were none around anywhere "in those parts". We pulled the old lifter out and one of the mechanics, having mercy on us, cleaned the sticky parts. We put everything back together and our hopes were high. It was day six, and we were getting tired of getting up literally with the cows in the pasture. We tried to start the car, but it wouldn't start. *However,* it did not backfire into the carburetor!

Disgusted and a bit disheartened, we started replacing electrical parts. On the third try replacing things, the car started. The coil had burned out.

So a hydraulic lifter had frozen up and then the coil had burned out. We had our car back and I had *not* blown the engine!

We washed up, packed up our tent and stuff, and headed home. Our parents were quite concerned, too, and wanted us back. Now when that car started, there was a tick, tick, tick in it from the lifter, but it was running. This is where youth kicked in again.

Worried that the lifter, etc. would stick or break again, we decided to keep our speed down to fifty miles an hour. The engine seemed most comfortable at that speed. We also decided to drive *nonstop* as much as possible to get home, each of us sleeping four hours on, four hours off!

Wyoming to Connecticut – we made it home – tick, tick, tick and all! Over all, we traveled 7000 miles.

Shortly thereafter, I replaced all the lifters and pushrods (I was an expert now) and that car would take me on my honeymoon just a year later!

We were proud of ourselves, able to get home on our own. I like to think that that trip helped build our character and confidence as we moved on. We did it the hard way, but we pulled it off.

Chuckle 17

Why does it take so long for the motor to start when a thunderstorm is coming??

Manitoba tourist information place- we bought antlers here to take home!

Chapter 18

I Get Married
(And Unmarried!)

In the fall of 1965, I started dating seriously. Mrs. Minor introduced me to this cute gal, and soon after I was engaged. The following summer I was married to Ann Mycka of Southington. Using the good old '57 Oldsmobile, we honeymooned at Williamsburg, Virginia. Obviously, fishing took a break, while I switched majors and finished college, which took another year and a half. If it hadn't been for her, I would have dropped out. My wife worked in Hartford, so I bicycled daily to New Britain for my courses – newlywed energy!

After finishing my degree I became an elementary teacher in Hartford. I remember squeezing in a few fishing times even in those hectic days and Ann was a good sport. As cold as opening day was, she went fishing with me but I don't think it was the fish she loved! Anyway, I outfitted the front half of my little boat with metal hoops and covered them with clear plastic using clips. This kept the wind and spray from my wife and the crowning piece became a cooler full of grinders and a thermos of hot chocolate!

We hit Twin Lakes and Wononskopumuc both during those days. We must have looked strange, but we didn't care as she stayed warm in the plastic bubble.

During this time I met a professor named Dr. Scull. He ran trips for junior high kids in the summer, sponsored by the YMCA. He would take them to the upper Midwest, and to some of the great national parks like Yellowstone. He was looking for counselors and it didn't pay much, but when he said I could take Ann, my wife, I jumped aboard. Ann was pregnant, too.

Anyway, with five counselors, a bus, and a van, we took forty boys out West for six weeks. I was in charge of the fishing stuff. We canoed into the wilderness in Ely, Minnesota, and eventually ended up in the Yellowstone – Teton area. I rented a boat on Yellowstone Lake, and took the kids fishing in small groups. We did a lot of rowing, but *every* child caught a trout, mostly cutthroat trout and they hit the F5 frog Flatfish – shhhh!

Some of us climbed the Tetons, too. I have a picture of our group on a glacier. We even learned how to repel down cliffs in climbing school.

Sometimes there are *minor* things that get in the way of fishing; things like school, college, getting married, or raising children. But this does not diminish the lure of the out-of-doors. It only delays or pauses the fun and I began to share that fun with my family. My first son, Christopher, was born in November, 1969, and then son Shaun came in December of 1971. The Lord truly blessed me, and as the kids grew, I worked more and more, holding down two jobs for the next twenty-one plus years. But there were two things I never missed. One was opening day, the other was vacations and no matter what, we met those goals. As the kids grew, we all looked forward to these times. Vacations bond families together, and fishing kept me sane!

The excitement of opening day began to build as winter left and early spring warmed the waters. We always worried that the third Saturday in April would come before ice out, but usually everything was open by then. The four of us somehow managed to enjoy a twelve foot boat.

And vacations became highlights too, and although I worked two jobs, painting and teaching, we still went north for a few weeks every year. Those mountains gave me enough strength and peace to carry me through family obligations. Vacations provided valuable down time to unwind and recharge. We built makeshift docks, we fished, we swam, we skied (grandpa and grandma camped too with their boat), and we explored. Campfires and bike rides capped off our fun activities.

The boys began to branch toward their own interests, and I quickly found out that bringing them both fishing together wasn't always wise. As brothers do, there were spats here and there, so I occupied the middle seat sometimes. Chris was older and more intense and took to fishing with vigor. Shaun was more laid back and younger and would rather do things his way, like play in the water off the back of the boat. But they both had their Old Pal tackle boxes at the ready.

As Shaun grew he developed a fondness for boating and skiing, and we got a canoe at one point, which he loved. He would paddle all over the place, taking his mother or me for rides. At a later time we had a small sailboat, and Shaun mastered sailing a bit too. He also made a big four foot circle out of plywood and painted it red. He skied with it behind Grandpa's boat, and even placed a chair on it, which he stood on as he skied. We were all impressed when he tried a ladder on his giant ski circle and mastered that too. Patience and perseverance have done him well over the years.

Chris could ski too, but also took to northern pike fishing. He became pretty good at it and would often bring one in from the lake that was a keeper. Yes, they got old enough to run the motor and his secret lure was the Rapala countdown – gold or silver.

Their mother Ann became good at it too and on one lucky day, on Follensby Clear Pond, she took three northerns over thirty inches each. All were caught on the M2 gold or silver Flatfish! We thought we really struck gold with that lure, but as time and other lures popped up, we tried other things. The M2's faded into the background but they are still in my tackle collection.

To this day, I still enjoy that campground. To complete the circle, in the spring of 2008, my son Shaun brought his wife Jennifer and their son Finley to enjoy the camping and fishing there too. The fourth generation, splashing off the dock! And in 2009, Shaun and Jenn were blessed with daughter Grace Mae!

Sometime in these early married years, I met a guy at work named John Bernetich. John was a science teacher and fished too, so we sort of traded similar stories. We ended up fishing at Lakeville together, me wanting to show him how well the giant M2 Flatfish worked. And it worked some, pretty well. At this time John showed me a new technique called "the jig-and-pig" and stocking up on pork rinds soon followed.

I do remember that we did sneak in an ice fishing outing several times, too. We went to Twin and also to the Plainville Reservoir. The reservoir was memorable because we were too stubborn and eager to fish, and probably should have gone home. Anyway, we fished, but the ice was *thin*. It would crack under our feet, and we could not get near each other for fear of the ice breaking. The small Rapala ice jig worked very well, but John finally gave (smartly) into common sense, and we quit early. He says, to this day, he would never do that again! I guess our angels were on duty that day, too.

During one of those rare trips, John asked if I wanted to go more. Sadly, I had to decline, since I had kids and part-time work and all. John understood, realizing family obligations must come first. Little did I know that John and I would become great fishing buddies some twenty years down the road. He got transferred to another building at work, but we would eventually seek fish and adventure again, as time passed.

As the kids grew and branched out into different interests, I kept working. This was sort of the "trickle" fishing period. We never missed opening day though, and once in a while we would get away.

I remember one time, in the spring in late April or early May, Chris and I were fishing at Lakeville. We were trolling minnows with that special rig. Chris was using my South Bend ultra light rod and reel with four pound test line. We were moving along a drop-off on the northwest shoreline, twelve to fourteen feet deep when Chris yelled, "I got one!"

I could see that and I reeled in quickly and grabbed the net, all the while giving directions. "Keep the pole bent, don't point it, and loosen some of the drag!", I exclaimed.

He did a perfect job, and after what seemed forever, we landed the fish. At eleven years old he handled a 6.25 pound, twenty-two inch brown on four pound test line.

Of course, when we came in, his pride was showing, and people noticed. Somehow, a photographer showed up and Chris's picture ended up in the local paper. Good for him and good for another nice day of fishing! Chris's picture hung in the boathouse for a number of years later.

For camping we ended up with a small pop-up camper when the kids were small. After baby Chris fell out of the end of it and onto the ground, we moved up to a nineteen foot self-contained used camp trailer. I named it "Poke Slow", since I didn't go too fast with it. Those old cars (an Electra 225 at this point) tended to heat up fast with speed. We camped quite a bit on the weekends, hitting Housatonic Meadows State Park, Austin Hawes Campground, Black Rock State Park, and sometimes Hammonasset State Park. I would fish Lakeville from the Housatonic campground, but most times we would just enjoy camping. I now live close enough to walk to one of those campgrounds (Black Rock State Park).

A bit frustrated trying to get fishing, I started another hobby that has proved quite enjoyable. In order to "stick around camp", so to speak, and help with the kids, I started identifying wildflowers. I always wanted to be able to go through the woods and know the names of what I was passing. I learned, and gained much knowledge and confidence and then had another bright idea!

I began to cross reference the flowers with edible wild plant books. Nice! Now I could identify wild edible food, and I did. And God bless a tolerant mother.

During this time she came down with a bad cold. Yup! I had the remedy. I took some wild leaves, boiled them, then poured the broth through gauze to take out the hairs, and I had a warm cure for colds. Mom reluctantly but lovingly tried some… and got better! I was a healer but no one else cooperated!

The work and joy of raising our kids and general obligations took most of my time during the next fifteen years or so. I fished when I could, and enjoyed my family and job in Hartford. I often worked nights and Saturday's painting, too. Then in 1986 –1987, I hit a rocky road. After twenty-one years married, I went through an amicable divorce, as we put our kids first. During this time, my fishing friends helped me along greatly, and I leaned on them for support and solace.

As a result, I began to fish with them more and more as things smoothed out. Steve O'Hara and John Bernetich began to play a bigger and bigger role in my life and fish we did. At this time, I moved to Forestville,CT.

Things are always tough at times like these, and fishing did fill a void. On Christmas day, a year or two after, I was to see the kids later in the day, so I went fishing in the morning. Being home alone was not desirable, and my parents were in Florida, my brother lived in New York.

I went to Hamlin's Pond in Plainville and wow, the fish were biting. Merry Christmas! In a few hours, I had my limit of trout, fishing through the ice, and they were good-sized. I swung by my friend John's house, proudly displayed my catch, and went home and cleaned fish before the kids arrived. Santa was nice to distract me that day and I was probably only one of very few fishermen to limit out on Christmas morning.

I started bringing my twelve foot boat back to the Hogback Reservoir. The following fall, I took a chance I probably shouldn't have. Johnny Muller, Warren's brother, wanted to go out trout fishing on the reservoir with me, but when we met there the wind was howling.

Now, John's a pretty muscular guy, so he decided it was too rough for two of us in a small boat. Whitecaps were blowing off the tops of the waves, as he tried to convince me not to go, too. I stupidly decided to go anyway. We launched the boat, motor, equipment, and all, and I rowed out and quickly started the motor. I had rain gear on, and headed up wind against the waves. In no time, I was soaked with spray and the boat was slapping big waves as I left Johnny behind.

The water was really cold and I knew there was no way to survive if a mistake was made, life jacket or not. I had to grab the oar with one hand to hold the bouncing gas can in the front of the boat. It seemed the boat was almost ready to blow over backward! With the other hand I ran the little motor. I prayed it would not quit and I could not turn around, the waves were too big.

I made my way slowly up wind and finally got to the Colebrook dam that blocked the wind and gave me shelter. Relieved, and thankful for the skills I had learned over the years, I was happy the motor never failed. I was whipped but after bailing the boat, I fished a good part of the day in the lieu of the upper dam. I got several trout and once the wind went down, I made my way back to the launch area. Johnny and his wife Sue were there when I arrived. They were relieved to see me and were concerned all day. I got wiser that day, as they help me pack up, and I was thankful that the Lord hadn't called me home. I had tested fate, and had no desire to do that again.

That "Bud's Buddy" boat got around. I brought it to the Adirondacks the following August. I went up for a week because my friend Warren wished to bring his son Matt there to show him around. He drove almost nonstop from San Diego, and his brother Bob, who lived in Bristol, joined us there too. Uncle Bob and Matt rented a boat, and Warren and I used mine. We enjoyed the lakes and fishing, and the general horsing around. When Bob and Matt decided to challenge us to a rowing race back to camp, we met their challenge. Now those guys are strong, and as Warren rowed us to victory, Bob and Matt (Bob rowed) were close behind. Bob's power however snapped the oar, and we ended up paying for a new set of oars at the rental. Unexpected outcomes always seem to accompany horsing around!

Chuckle 18

We must teach our wives that nets are not clubs!

Chris's 6.25lb., 22 inch Brown Trout; Lakeville, CT.

Shaun skiing on his homemade disc!

Chapter 19

I Get a Bigger Boat
Out of State Lakes

Around this time I realized-duh-I needed a bigger boat. After looking around, I settled on a sixteen foot Grumman with walk through seats and a deep bow. I bought an outboard at Larry's Marine Works in Forestville, CT. I started hanging out there after work, and picked up valuable information and fishing tips, as well as friendships.

Larry DeSimone became a good friend and gave me a great deal on a twenty-five horsepower Johnson motor. I got just the basics, but when we picked it up (it was shipped to a Plainville factory), it was equipped with an electric starter. I told him I didn't order that and couldn't afford it but he told me to pay for it over time and take as long as I wished.

You know, he was a wise fellow. I was older now, and pull starting a big motor is no fun. I have always been thankful for his wisdom. You push the button, bang, it starts. How easy and wonderful. When I hit my seventies, I'll consider a power lift, too!

Anyway, I started to fish a lot again, both with Steve O'Hara and John Bernetich. John had an apartment in Plainville, and I stopped there quite often after work. We ended up planning many "expeditions" together, and traded all sorts of tales and we still fish together today.

It was John who eventually named my boat. I like fishing reels and poles, and usually take four to six when I fish as I hate tying knots. It's quicker to just grab a different pole. So I bought reels from time to time. John noticed, and when I suggested I was going to name my boat, he came up with "Reel Happy". And it seemed to fit and my boat was named.

John introduced me to a lake near Colchester, called Hayward Lake. He often ice fished it after work, and we started going there quite regularly. We got many panfish out of the north cove.

We went there one winter when there was quite a wind blowing, and Steve joined us. I put up a wind block wall using aluminum poles and eventually, the wind bent my poles right over! We learned we better use ropes.

In those days I was using an ice chopper (spud) that my brother made for me. It had a stainless steel sharpened block on the bottom that held a nice sharp edge. The handle was a threaded pipe and I had about a six foot rope on it.

Well, about midday, Steve was making a new hole and, as has happened to countless fishermen before, the ice chopper went down the hole; all by itself, of course. We were in about ten feet of water.

After inventorying our lures, we found a Daredevil and started jigging for the rope and we finally had success! Apparently, the chopper acted like a harpoon, and stuck straight up in the mud. We got the rope and pulled her up and I still have that spud today, and use it to chop sidewalk ice. Learning from my mistakes, however, I put on a much longer rope till I finally bought an auger!

Augers are great improvements over choppers. On my fiftieth birthday, my friends chipped in on a power auger. For years afterward, we made the ice look like Swiss cheese, and effortlessly drilled all the holes we needed.

Steve and I started to fish together a lot, especially up north. He and I started to get real interested in fishing for lake trout, especially in Saranac Lake, N.Y. Connecticut once had lake trout, in Lakeville (Wononskopomuc), but eutrophication from fertilizers seem to have killed them off. The Connecticut record is 29 lbs. 13 oz. caught in 1918 by Dr. Thompson. There are no other places in Connecticut for lakers, although I think Colebrook River Lake or perhaps Candlewood Lake might be able to support them. I'm sure the authorities would know.

Anyway, we decided to get serious and chased lakers and some browns for years. We started out with downriggers and downrigger poles. Some guys at Larry's had fished Quabbin and had good luck on Sutton spoons, especially the hammered tin size 44 silver. Now Sutton spoons, made in Maples, New York, aren't cheap, and come silver plated. I started ordering spoons of all sizes from Larry on a pretty consistent basis over the next five years or so and finally dedicated a whole tackle box to them. Larry thought I was cornering the market but they work real well for trout.

So, Steve and I upgraded to heavier portable downriggers, and started pulling Sutton spoons in deep Saranac water. And we started catching some lakers. It usually took about four hours to catch one, but we were persistent. We really got to know the lake well and I added a small used six horsepower motor to my boat, so I could troll at slow speeds.

It didn't take long for us to begin pulling lead line, too. On each ten yards of lead line, the color of the line changes. Each color out drops the lure about ten feet or so, and we got good at skimming the bottom. Lakers like the bottom. We used various pumping techniques, and whenever one of us got a fish, the pump pattern was of course copied.

I also used the lead line rig in both Twin Lakes and Lakeville. I would troll either Suttons or minnows at thirty-five or forty feet and it usually produced great action. I suppose streamers would have worked too, never enough time!

As we got better we started fiddling with the lures. Yep – "doctored" those things. The Sutton size 72 started working well. It was a bigger lure and we put feathers on the hooks, and stuck eyes on the blades.

I also started bringing my small boat along (on the roof of my van), so we could get into smaller lake trout lakes. One such lake was Hoel Pond, and Steve and I both took a laker out of there that was over sixteen pounds in July of '89 and July of '90. Both were taken on downriggers at about fifty feet or so.

Eventually, we went with just lead line poles, and phased out the heavier downriggers. A few times up north we got our limit (three) of lakers, and to this day, laker fishing is one of my favorite things to do. Lake trout can get real big!

Steve and I went after some brown trout and landlocks also. We found that the "locals" were using a lure called The Hinkley, made by the Elmer Hinkley Company of New York. A few were sold locally in New York, and we had great luck with them. We were catching trout up to five pounds. We especially grew fond of Lake Colby in the town of Saranac, and took browns and Landlock salmon rather consistently. The lure worked well. It was tin colored, skinnier than a Mooseluk, and had models up to five inches long. It probably resembled a smelt. There were so few sold in the area and they worked so well that we bought them all up! We figured that way they would only work for us. How naïve!

Year after year, hour after hour, we trolled and eventually stumbled onto our next phase. I am still in this phase today, even in Connecticut, so keep this info just between us. Somewhere around 1998, while pulling lead line over a favorite area in Saranac, Steve and I could see fish in some numbers on the bottom. After many passes and no fish, we decided that we would stop and jig for those fish. Our hunch was that we were seeing smallmouths.

I had just been introduced to the three and a half inch tube jig, and we decided those fish could be tempted. In no time, I hooked a heavy fish and lost it. I hooked a second fish and lost that one too. The wire hook had straightened out. The same thing happened a third time and I decided to try a big one ounce jig with a heavy-duty hook. Bam! The hook held and we boat-ed it! It wasn't a small mouth – it was a nice laker. We were dancing. Our whole world and way of thinking changed. We took three lakers that day in very little time – on jigs!

On our return during the following years we began to have good success jigging up lake trout. And so, of course, I stocked up on tube lures and one ounce saltwater jigs. I painted them myself. One can throw them a mile and work a big area if one is patient. We used fourteen to seventeen pound monofilament line. I even bought extra anchor rope so I could let out twenty-five feet at a time to cover large areas without starting the motor (with my electric starter!).

I also added an electric motor for rather calm days so I could either hold or move quietly to cover ground. This technique has paid off great dividends of nice fish. Eventually I added a high-quality Lowrance fish finder and the setup was complete.

It makes sense to fish where the fish are, and not just troll through them. I used to keep my catch, but now a quick photo suffices, and back in the water they go; more about lakers later.

I enjoyed many years of fishing in New York with Steve. We hit Whey Pond and had great success catching nice rainbows on chenille jigs! John, Steve, and I also fished Paradox Lake, Brant Lake, and Eagle Lake north of Lake George.

On one trip to Vermont, Steve and I joined John Bernetich and his friend Ken Bragg on a trip to the Hero Islands on Lake Champlain. We wanted to "clobber" smallmouths. John had a bigger boat with more power, good for Champlain. Steve and I followed him around, since he knew the lake, and we all had adequate success.

Steve did unusually well. He caught a *seagull* on his Rapala in the middle of a perch school. Have you ever seen someone playing a seagull! It's half funny; half "I don't know what to do". He eventually got the bird to John's boat where John put the bird under his arm, unhooked it, and let it go! We dubbed Steve "Bird King".

On the last fishing day we went on the eastern side of the lake and the wind was really up. John and Ken headed out, and we tried to follow, but the waves were pretty big and poor Steve was getting banged around in the front of my smaller boat. After twenty or thirty minutes or so of pounding, we turned around and fished elsewhere, in sheltered areas.

This trip had consequences because when I got home I noticed star cracks around the front upper rivets of my boat. I had the boat inspected (it was warranteed) and after much ballyhoo, they admitted there was a flaw in the design. The boat flexes around the front seat brackets, causing the cracks. They replaced my boat and allowed me to pick out another nice (better actually) sixteen foot boat –The Walleye Wonder. I still use that boat today but after ten plus years, the warranty has run out. That boat has served me very well.

When not going to the Adirondacks, I started fishing more and more with John. Of course, several times we made the "we couldn't resist" trip to Mexico, Oswego, and Selkirk in New York. We got nice big browns and were intrigued with the steelhead guys. And, of course, if one wasn't careful, one could empty one's wallet on the latest "hot" lures. Getting wiser, I didn't bite – well, not too hard, anyway. Our bight jointed Rapalas worked a-okay.

Now, my brother Hal and his wife Susan moved to New York, to a place on Point Peninsula named Three Mile Bay west of Watertown. They took a shell of a log cabin and turned it into a beautiful "Ponderosa", restoring the house and property right on the shores of Lake Ontario. John and I landed there, with his bigger boat, and we fished.

We launched at Henderson Harbor and went after perch. More and more, John and I moved toward panfish fishing, and we had great success on the bottom of that harbor. We nailed big perch on the three and a half inch (lighter) tube jig. It was becoming very dependable.

John and I had other trips too. We wanted to become walleye fisherman and heard that Oneida Lake was walleye territory. So John, Ken, and I decided to ice fish the place. We rented an ice shack and the place towed it and our gear way out onto the lake. They even drilled holes for us. They also made the comment that they never saw people with so much equipment!

When we rented the shack, we asked about lures, and they showed and sold us the local special. The homemade lure was called the Sewer Pipe and was made from a piece of pipe hammered out and painted. It was supposed to vibrate and attract walleyes. Off we went with the local special!

Well, we fished all day, and had a good time with our shack, fishing through holes in the floor and drilling more holes outside. One could hardly see land from where we were. We caught nothing, but our food was good.

We later learned that the shack was not really positioned in the right place. There is structure way out there where walleyes "play" and we were off to the side a football field or more. We were the strangers you know! And that secret local lure? I think they saw us coming – winter fun on a slow day.

John and Ken returned there again at another time, and John and I fished Oneida on one summer trip also. We never did hit significant walleyes but did manage some nice bass. Oneida is the only place where we have observed smallmouth and largemouth bass working together to herd baitfish! That's the only time I have ever seen that. And John got only one walleye on a leech.

Fishing with either Steve, or John, the poor fish didn't have a chance. One of us would usually figure out what works to catch fish.

In 1993 the boy's mother died of leukemia after a valiant battle, and my attention became focused even more on them. Both were in college and exhibited tremendous courage and poise at this time. I admired their strength and endurance as they coped with a tough situation. Shaun graduated from Bentley College and Chris got his degree from UCONN. Their mother would have been so proud, as am I.

Chuckle 19

Ever get behind a person at a launch that needs lessons on how to back up a boat?!!

Chapter 20

Someone Catches Me

Over the years my friend John became a bit well-known in our circles for hosting an annual ice fishing party. He held it on Winchester Lake, and his friend Ken and I helped. We'd set up tents, flags, stoves, and would bring plenty of firewood for the "big fire". I remember pulling five sleds of all kinds of equipment across the lake at one time and, boy, did we go home tired! Many people were invited, with the emphasis of course on females. Yes, John talked some ladies out onto the ice, too. Some worried the ice would break, so we would gladly hold their hands and gently walk them out on the ice. We'd cross the lake, and bring them to our setup.

We loved it when the ice all of a sudden would let out a loud crack! Oh, oh, time for hugs of reassurance! The ladies always wondered why the fire never burned a hole in the ice but we always had at least ten inches of ice, and everyone had a good time. And we sure enjoyed the food.

One of the guys that came got pretty teed- off at me once when I told him where he could take a leak, around the corner. When he came back, he had put one leg through the ice. I guess he went too far; to where a brook comes in. He hit a soft spot and was soaked. Wrong place I guess! I kind of made myself scarce checking tip-ups and re-baiting.

At another time, a few people got briefly lost in the woods looking for firewood but everyone brought great food, and we all feasted well. Quite often John and some others even stayed after dark.

Other people, whole families even, brought kids, and we showed them how tip-ups worked, or they would fly kites, toast marshmallows, skate, or try to drill a hole.

John did this for a number of years and of course the talk in the spring would shift to "which ladies are you inviting this year?" etc.

We were single guys, ya know, and for some reason not many fish were caught at those parties. We did catch conversation and fish stories were traded.

At this time of my life, my parents were spending winters in St. Petersburg, Florida. I made several trips down, and fished a few times from the shore at Fort Desoto. I was always amazed that giant egrets and herons would lurk just a few feet over one's shoulder, and eat any little fish you could catch. It was so enjoyable fishing waist deep in warm water in the middle of winter – a nice experience.

One motel I stopped at on a trip down seemed deserted and a bit sleazy. No one was there for more than a few hours?? It was cheap, but I slept with the tire iron that night – and made a note to avoid that place the next time!

On one trip back, I hit a pretty good snowstorm in North Carolina and Virginia. They don't plow there like they do up north, and the road got covered quickly. I had a CB radio (remember those days) and listened in to truckers. They were swearing a blue streak because the ice and snow was forming potholes in the road. The jarring was shaking them so violently they complained their teeth were falling out!

I had an older Buick Electra 225. The heater core had gone a month before, and I painstakingly replaced it. A good deal of the dashboard had to be taken out to do so. I put it all back together and only had a few parts left over.

As I followed one of those tractor-trailers over those banging potholes, the whole dashboard on the passenger side began to sag and threatened to fall down. I thought about those left over parts!

I eventually exited the interstate and had to drive another fifty miles from the highway to find a room. They shut down the highway soon afterward. That was quite a trip, but I enjoyed fishing with those egrets.

During those winters, John and I ice fished a lot. We had many favorite spots, as all fishermen do, and developed favorite techniques and lures. We were having luck with tip-ups (flag!) and jigged Rapalas and Swedish Pimples.

On one outing, we were able to get into Long Pond (Wanonpakook) in Salisbury, Connecticut. It is the sister lake south of Wononskopomuc, and had good bass and calico fishing. That day there were three of us – John, his friend Tim, and I. The ice was a little iffy but it was cold and about five inches seemed okay. In overcast with flurries, we walked down the western side of the lake and set out tip-ups. Then we decided to get some firewood to add to what we brought, and went in toward shore. John found some downed wood, and Tim was ahead of me when – wow – three feet from shore he fell in! His feet and pants got soaked. I got lucky, he was ahead of me. We later saw there was a small flow from shore at that location, making the ice thin.

We built a fire and hung his clothes on branches to dry. I had retrieved some clothes from my van for him to put on, and he stayed by the fire and fished there. But, hours later, as he moved around, he slipped in the water made by the fire and fell, with one foot going into the fishing hole. He was wet again!

We kept the fire going, and finished the day. At day's end, Timmy lost a very big bass on one of his tip-ups as he wrestled it up. The fish had taken almost all his line out and it was a shame he lost it. We got some nice bass out of that lake. John told me a few weeks later that Tim was out of work with pneumonia. We felt pretty bad, but Tim wasn't to be talked out of leaving a fishing trip, even though we tried. That became a tough winter for him, and we became a bit wiser about checking for safe ice.

The power auger allowed us to move around more on the lakes, and, as we moved, we seemed to catch more fish. Eventually we phased out most of the tip-ups, and just took multiple jigging poles. I still have all my well-made tip-ups today (half are Dad's), but they sit in a corner waiting for kids or grandchildren to use. There is something special about the excitement of someone yelling "Flag!" and seeing everyone run to an ice hole with curious anticipation. Fishermen always wonder what's going to come through the hole.

We started fishing mainly for panfish. Oh, we caught good bass, trout, and pickerel occasionally, but threw them back. We liked bluegills, perch, and calico bass, and filleted them up for meals often. And as our movements changed, so did our lure choices.

More often than not, some new lure would appear on the end of one of our lines, and we enjoyed surprising each other. One type of lure that began to intrigue us was the chenille jig. It started working well for both perch and calico, and I bought many color combinations. Pink and white worked well, then yellow and black, then red and white, on and on. We also changed weights – one-sixteenth of an ounce, one thirty-second of an ounce, etc., until I had another tackle box or two filled with chenille jigs of all colors and weights. Now, there is only so much time on a lake, and the lures outnumbered the times to use them. And we all know if something is working, you stick with it, and you don't try new colors. Many chenille lures still sit waiting in my box! They also worked during open water fishing, too. We even gave them original names, like "the Bumblebee", or "Pinky".

During winter we returned to Mudge Pond often because it seemed colder and had safer ice. The south bay and western shore would produce for us early in the season. Then we would fish shallow water in the north as the season drew to a close. We once saw several guys catch about fifty big perch right out in the middle of the lake in twenty feet of water, using the Rapala jig.

We also hit West and East Twin Lake. I liked West Twin (the middle pond) the best because the calico were easier to find. We liked the drop-offs as you go west from the "Between the Lakes Road", about one fourth of the way across. We also had luck toward the west shore of the "middle" lake, too.

We made many trips there, and one stands out particularly. One day I went to West Twin Lake and parked in a cul-de-sac off the Between the Lakes Road. I walked down through some woods and onto the lake. I drilled multiple nine inch holes with the power auger in eight to ten feet of water off the western shore. I hit many calicos and was pleased with my day.

When I got home, I told John, and we eagerly returned the next day. It had snowed several inches at night, but we trekked out with no problem. As we were setting up, I was about to tell John to be careful of the old holes when – yup – down he went with one leg into a snow-camouflaged old hole. One boot full of water, one mouthful of expletives! Off I went for spare socks and shoes kept in the van. I sheepishly knew I should have warned him earlier.

We also continued to bang away at Hayward Lake when there was safe enough ice. The perch and gills were big.

Wanting to extend the ice fishing season, we finally decided that we would fish up north, in Massachusetts, for many more weeks each year. And so we did.

Massachusetts has some nice lakes, and they weren't that far away. We tried Otis but one lake that John's friend, Dave Gauthier, told us about was Garfield Lake in Monterey. The area is cooler due to the elevation (at about 1200 ft.), and we started fishing there on a regular basis. The bluegills and perch were firm and big, and we hit trout, two, accidentally. We had many fine trips and enjoyed the Berkshire surroundings.

Overtime our lure choices changed again. We not only went tiny, but we began to experiment with two and four pound test monofilament line. A few new lures we uncovered (our ears and eyes were always open) were the silver teardrop lure and the Rat Finke. The Rat Finke in chartreuse or hot pink worked very well, and we have used them successfully now for many years. The teardrop lures in many colors (and some with tiny blades) sometimes "killed them" too! We now even use them in the summer with or without bobbers and another small tackle box was created.

In the winter we fished Garfield off Sylvan Road in the eastern part of the lake. Access was kind of tough but worth it. When spring arrived we fished Garfield by boat, but the launch is open only *before* Memorial Day and *after* Labor Day. It is closed in the summer.

It was on Garfield that I finally burned out my twenty-five horsepower Johnson motor. Repair said it was too "used up" to fix, so I bought a twenty-five horse four cycle Yamaha the next spring, of course with an electric start! It is a nice motor and gets great mileage.

I mentioned before that Garfield was sometimes hard to get into. On one day we were there after a snow, and decided to walk in from the main road. It is about a quarter-mile walk or so around a bay with a stream flowing down the middle. We stayed on the north side, and oops, John became a "mudder". I stayed just offshore, John was in closer. The ice and fifteen inch snow wasn't holding him, and his boots kept coming up with mud, lots of mud. Now, walking on snow, with thin ice and mud below is no fun. The shoreline had some springs, and John found a few. He made his way along and eventually found firm footing as we made our way to the main lake. I had lucked out again. John was beginning to think that maybe I should lead the way in the future!

John and I also fished Goose Pond, another Dave suggestion. Ice fishing wasn't very good but in open water, if one knows where, Goose has big bluegills and some nice smallmouths. We usually fished the second lake, through a nice little stream. Most people fished Goose for trout, and the clear water holds some beauties.

We ventured into both Big Benton and Little Benton Lakes, too. There is a nice stream from the boat launch to Big Benton Lake, about a half-mile long or so and when the leaves are turning, it's a beautiful ride. We also fished Thousand Acre Pond, north of Norfolk, a few times, too.

Around this time, John began to do some country and western dancing, and dating came on the scene. During these times, John encouraged me to get into country dancing too. After much resistance, I finally relented when he sold me a pair of boots that didn't fit him. It was a great deal at twenty-five dollars and they were a good fit for me. That twenty-five dollar investment changed my life.

I went for lessons, and eventually ended up at the Illusions dance hall, in Wolcott, CT. At one time when they were teaching a new dance everyone was taken or partnered up during the lesson. I guess the girls knew I had two left feet. Well, this cute lady slid onto the seat next to me, and said she'd dance with me, but she had a bad foot. Her name was Cindy and we enjoyed each other's company, *and* she had a son who was a bass fisherman!

I went on vacation shortly afterward, and couldn't shake feelings stirring inside. Poor Steve O'Hara – I made him cut a vacation a bit short and drive home in the rain, so I could go dancing at the Cadillac Ranch in Plainville the next day. I was really hoping to bump into Cindy again. And so I did! She was there and we danced maybe once or twice, then got a booth and talked and talked. Actually we closed the place!

My angel named Cindy even put up with me having no rhythm at all. I practiced and practiced those dances, both at home and during breaks at work – one, two, and three – kick, ball, chain – whatever. I cassette-taped country and western songs, pulled my curtains, and danced like a fool all over my apartment learning those moves. I was in love!

After a time and many dances, we were engaged, and finally married in November, 1997. We both think the other was heaven-sent, and have enjoyed our lives ever since. Quite quickly, dancing was phased out of the picture but it had accomplished its mission.

Cindy lived in Thomaston, and I moved there, within walking distance of Black Rock State Park, the place I bicycled to many years before. If you remember I mentioned that when I was small Dad almost always had to take his second choice of picnic spots at Point

Folly on Bantam Lake. We are pretty sure it was Cindy's Dad that always got his cooler on that first choice picnic spot.

Shortly after this John bought a house in East Hampton. He located closer to the saltwater since he fished on Long Island Sound too. I could not go on saltwater, since I get sea sick.

The first trip I took Cindy on was to my beloved Adirondacks and she caught a beautiful five pound brown trout. She wanted to see the Grand Canyon so we made two trips west. We drove the van to the Yellowstone area on one trip, and went to the Grand Canyon on a second trip. On the second trip, we continued on to San Diego where we visited Warren and his new wife Kit. His first wife Joanne had lost a long tough battle with breast cancer a few years earlier.

Cindy and I have always continued to visit the Adirondacks every year. Saranac Lake and those lakers always seemed to call me back and Cindy has developed her own fishing style.

Chuckle 20

When the wife's in the boat, how come she gets miffed, even though you beat the thunderstorm by ten seconds?

Chapter 21

Bad Shower, Big Fish

One great bonus I got when I married Cindy was a fishing stepson named Stephen. Steve is a great guy and he and his father fished avidly at this time and were good at it. They participated in bass tournaments, and were up on the latest thig-a-ma-jigs that worked. One can see where this is headed – more tackle!

Anyway, Steve introduced me to the great effects of tube jigs, and tipped me off as to the colors and sizes that were working. They worked very well and I still use them today, using various techniques.

Slowly, ever so slowly, I have coaxed a few good spots out of Stephen regarding Bantam Lake. He is an expert on that lake, since he grew up only ten miles away. I love "pumping" him for information, and he loves pretending not to know anything. Yeah! But he nicely relents (at times). And for me, even without tips, fishing around Point Folly was productive!

I started using those jig colors up north and became very successful with lake trout, using both the three and a half inch and the four inch size, too. I have always been grateful for his input.

A year after we were married, in August, Cindy and I went away for a few days to camp near Paradox Lake, New York. We ended up at a private campground, set up our screen house and slept in our van.

Poor Cindy, when she went to the shower, it was not nice. The building was the size of an outhouse, with a wood slat floor to let the water through, and it was small and smelly, and a bit slimy. There was one twelve inch florescent bulb and no sink. She was a trooper, but I felt bad we had to use such a facility. The campground was nice, the facilities were poor. We only stayed for a few days. The public campground up the street was full for the summer.

Well, we launched the boat and headed out for a nice day on Paradox Lake. It was partly sunny and warm, not too hot for an

August day. I had fished this lake with John and Steve O'Hara years earlier, and remembered structure somewhere in the middle of the lake. There is a small dome that rises in fifty feet of water. I headed that way, and casted a big tube jig in that area.

Within minutes I slammed into something big! Learning from the past, I always set the hook hard twice. I don't like to lose fish, so I either lose them at the beginning or not at all, as my philosophy goes. That fish would not come up. It ran, and I was running out of ten pound test line. With one hand I started the motor (good ol' electric start) and began slowly chasing the fish with the motor in reverse as I was losing line rapidly. Cindy picked up the net and stood ready, and we both got very excited. I kept repeating, "This is a big one, this is a big one…"

Pump, pump, slowly the fish started coming up. As the fish lunged many times it became weaker and gradually came closer. Slowly, up, up, up – closer it came. Cindy gasped as the big laker rolled to the surface. It was wrapped in my line and was slowly rolling and unwrapping on the surface. I could see the hook was very loose.

"Net it!" I cried. Cindy couldn't – she was too scared! A fish that size surprised her. I yelled for her to give me the net, and I slid it under the fish just in time. What a monster. We were jubilant. My biggest fish ever!

We quit fishing. This fish had to be weighed and put on ice. Running away, my ego was thinking;"maybe a state record!" At the dock, the rangers took pictures, people ooh-d and ahhh-ed, and we headed for our cooler at camp to ice the fish.

At a local tackle shop, they weighed the fish using some crude scale. They said it was twenty-three pounds, eleven ounces and about forty-three inches long. I think this scale was off on the low side, but they entered me into the local yearly fishing derby.

Checking in the following year, I had won a trophy from the Schroon Lake Chamber of Commerce for the biggest lake trout caught in 1998. That was nice and of course I thanked Cindy's son Stephen and his dad on the tip about tube jigs.

Cindy and I also visited Wellesley Island, in New York, and we trolled the St. Lawrence River hoping for muskies. We never hit any, but really enjoyed the Thousand Islands. One could spend a lifetime fishing and exploring there. That is one powerful, fascinating river, and we covered miles.

When John moved to East Hampton, we began concentrating on the area. John lived only ten miles from Hayward Lake so we began fishing it a lot. We were hitting giant calico bass in several locations on various trips, and we took plenty of panfish over the years. Because our freezer usually had fish, I began to only take ten or twelve panfish each trip. We most always threw the game fish (bass, trout) back.

One memorable moment came when I was at work and received a phone call from John. He had retired, and was happily ice fishing Hayward. He called me and rubbed it in pretty well, asking "How's work going, Ed?" and "Guess where I am?". I was already close to retirement and retired as soon as I was able, and we ice fish often now.

John also had access to Lake Pocotopaug, and we tried to get walleyes from there several times. We had no luck, but are still hopeful. At our age now, we tend to get to the lakes around 10 AM, and leave around 4 or 5 PM. Maybe that's why we don't catch walleyes that tend to feed at night or in the early morning. John and I enjoy jawing and talking about who knows what and it's become another wonderful part of fishing. We get to the lake whenever we get there and of course, with our skill, we're convinced that we can catch fish at any time. Well, that philosophy may need adjusting, since some days go begging! But we do okay and really enjoy each other's company.

Cindy and I continued to vacation at Fish Creek in the Adirondacks. On one trip to Upper Saranac Lake, I began the meticulous and involved process of teaching her how to jig for lake trout. Now Cindy is her own person, but she listened politely and attentively. I explained how to cast the jig far and leave the bail open until it sinks. I told her to watch the line, quickly raise the pole, reel in, and then let it sink again. I told her to pull if she sees a twitch or feels anything.

Cindy didn't like a long rod, so she used a shorter stiffer bass pole. Anyway, she got the technique down, and I turned to fish myself.

In no time, Cindy was jigging like crazy. Ignoring all my "expert" advice she exclaimed she wanted to do it her way. Being older and wiser now, I just smiled and shrugged. She was jigging straight down, going up and down quickly a foot or so at a time. Fifteen minutes later, I hear, "I think I got a fish!"

And, son of a bee…, she's pulling up a laker, a nice laker! Now I figure she must have driven that thing so crazy that it hit the jig just to kill it.

I still successfully fish my way, but Cindy, using her "nuclear chicken" technique lands her share of nice lakers, too. She's her own gal, and I'm very proud of her, as she proved everyone has their own approach to this wonderful sport. She keeps pace with me. So what do I know?

Chuckle 21

If you promise to be home by six, why do the fish start biting at five? "It's true dear!"

Our 23 pound, 11 ounce laker taken in Paradox Lake, N.Y.

Chapter 22

I Retire; Get to Know Other Lakes & Bantam

Once I retired in 2002, I fished on quite a regular basis, often once a week. Sometimes I would go out alone, and I enjoy that. When alone I can experiment with other crazy theories and lures, and explore spots I rarely go. And I'm not above just cruising around either, enjoying my boat (I wonder how fast it will go?). I find that I fish differently when alone, too, staying in places of interest much longer than normal and at least I don't waste anyone's time.

At other times I would join John or take Cindy or my son Chris. Son Shaun was in Downers Grove near Chicago, raising a family. With John in East Hampton, we explored Bashan Lake, a beautifully clear lake, and Gardner Lake stocked with walleyes. We know they're in there somewhere! We also ice fished Moodus a lot and became good panfish catchers.

Because of the great luck I had with big tube jigs, I figured that maybe the little ones would work well also. I sent away for smaller sizes and found that the two inch ones worked very well. They catch anything that eats minnows, and work well through the ice too. Perch, pickerel, bluegill, calico, trout, and bass – all are susceptible and I quickly filled another plastic box with various small sizes and colors. We even got into lures called Gitzits, a golden colored tube type lure (it comes in various other colors too). When tipped with a piece of worm or meal worm, all these jigs were extremely effective, and they became my number one panfish lure.

My stockpiles of lures that have been tested over time have been whittled down to fill just a view boxes – er – that go with me. At home, I have the "library of lures", so to speak, that are just too good to completely retire. One never knows when a new situation will need an old "workable" lure. Completely parting with old trusty lures is difficult, and like clothing styles, one never knows when something will work great again! Great excuse, eh!

John and I had a memorable trip to Mudge Pond late one fall during this period. We launched and started fishing in one of our favorite holes in the south bay. As we casted out, we noticed that our lines acted strangely. Usually when one casts, the line falls on the water but not this time. Instead, our lines made a big bow in the air and tried to rise up! We were amazed and baffled. There were a few flurries falling, but our lines were rising. We made numerous casts, and each time our lines tried to rise. Intrigued, John cut off his lure, and peeled out six to eight feet of line from the end of his pole. When he whipped it out over the water, the line rose in the air! We were bamboozled. Maybe heaven was calling us!

Another boat came by, and we asked them if they noticed the same phenomenon. They did, and were as perplexed as we were. They shrugged their shoulders as to an explanation. I have never seen that happen again, and we have theorized about it many times. An ordinary day that day sure turned quirky and memorable.

Every trip out has the potential to turn up some new idiosyncrasy or experience that makes it unique. And each new involvement entices us to the next trip; to go around the next corner, or to try a new lake or pond. Every trip always had something to offer, even if we didn't catch fish.

As probably most other fishermen have done, I studied stocking records over the years. Connecticut will release year old records – and they can give one some indication as to when and where fish are stocked. It increases one's chances to catch fish (not true!). I had charts for all of Connecticut and the northern New York counties, and the information was fun to go over during those doldrum winter months. I made graphs and charts, even when I was younger, and it was great math in the real world for a kid!

Anyway, now that I live in the computer age, I have learned how to graph on that "thing". I made a graph of the acreage of all the lakes I fish, just for practice, and to compare lake sizes. The possibilities for practice are obvious.

Lake Warmaug popped out at me one day as a lake that might have some potential. Cindy and I took a ride around the lake during the fall season, and she showed me around since she had camped there once. I noticed there was a crude, carry- in launch next to the beach at the state park. It wasn't long before I made plans.

I had long since sold the trailer to my small Starcraft boat, so I cleaned out our van and managed to slide the boat into it. It just fit inside.

Off I went, Warmaug bound, with my six horsepower 1968 Fishermen Evinrude and my "Bud's Buddy" boat. Now I was a bit annoyed that Warmaug had no boat launch, except for kayaks and canoes. I stopped dead in the road where the sign pointed to the launch, and rigged up portable wheels I had made for my boat. Long story short, it took over an hour to launch and set up. The lake was a bit far from the road and the minor traffic had to just go around me as best they could, in one open lane. But I didn't care and with eager effort, I set out to fish and explore.

I reversed the whole process when done. Getting out took more effort and time, since it was an uphill trek through sand with all the equipment. But I accomplished my mission. And the result of that mammoth effort; two small pickerel and one giant perch! But I had a very nice day! It's a pretty lake, but a state boat launch for trailers would be nice. The state of New York has almost every lake opened up, and Connecticut should do the same. The more lakes open, the more the fishermen are spread out.

I was always trying to come up with stuff that made things easier. We fished Hayward a lot, and the lake is an electric motors only lake – no gas engines. Some days it seemed it took forever to get around. Have you ever noticed that when you're fishing on one side of a lake, the other side looks better? "They are not hitting here, maybe it would be better over there!" often tumbled in my brain.

Now John's freshwater boat ironically is a sixteen foot "John boat". It has two heavy-duty handles in the front. And guess what I spotted in one of those trusty catalogs that somehow constantly arrived at my house? I found an adapter that would slide into the front boat handle and that would accommodate another electric motor! We bought it.

Between my electric motor and John's, we now had some speed. One motor pushed, one pulled, and we covered the lake in smart fashion. Of course we had to come to an agreement as to the same place to go – no problem. And maybe we gained ten more minutes of fishing time! Being older now, we are not the fastest guys on the lake, but we felt faster.

Because we're never in much of a hurry (now that's an understatement), we often found someone fishing in our favorite spot. At the discovery John would mumble "pond scum" and the term stuck. Someone fishing in our spot was termed "pond scum". That happened often, but we also realized that we, too, were "pond scum" to others. And so it was that John named his boat "Pond Scum". We kept on fishing, knowing that the best cure for "pond scum" was to find many good spots to fish. After all, you don't eliminate "pond scum"; you become "pond scum".

John often fished saltwater, but I couldn't, due to my tendency toward seasickness. However, we found a bit of a compromise when we tried fishing the Connecticut River. He used his bigger boat and we had great times. He showed me a great deal of the river as we launched at the Salmon River several times, and looked for bluefish. We explored Selden Creek and enjoyed passing Gillette Castle while motoring all the way to Hamburg Cove and beyond. We watched for birds feeding where blues were active and had great fun catching a few. Blues were quite a handful on lighter tackle. Cindy even got one when she went with us once.

In our earlier years when we chased bass we had also explored Candlewood Lake. Smallmouth fishing there is great and the better you know the lake, the more one catches, of course. We fished the northeast branch of the lake, hitting the deep edges of the weed beds, and had pretty good luck.

Because I lived so close to Bantam Lake, and I have a stepson that had "great" knowledge of the place, I began to fish it more and more. Now stepson Steve keeps things "close to the vest" so to speak, and as we bantered back and forth I gently coaxed one spot at a time out of him. I even "spied" on him a few times when we were both on the lake. And I loved pulling up to his boat while casually observing the lures attached to his poles. He was always a great sport about it.

Anyway, Bantam is a treasure. I found that white perch loved my lures and I could take a dozen good ones home most times. Calico bass were abundant, too, if one fished around deeper rocks.

The south bay produced white perch and calico also, but every once in a while we bumped into pretty big northern pike and smallmouths. Bantam has nice northerns, and sometimes they take jigs and bass lures.

My son Chris had some luck casting deep diver bass lures in the bay near the Point Folly store and launch. He got several nice pike and over near Deer Island he hooked the biggest largemouth I have ever seen. It came about three feet out of the water and threw the lure!

I'm still learning the lake and find the old adage still true. Find structure, find fish but it helps to know where the structure is ahead of time.

When the kids were little, my friend Bob Muller tipped us off to a special place near Bantam. Between the entrance to Point Folly and the bridge where the Bantam River leaves the lake, there is a hill to the northwest of the road. That hill that overlooks the bay is said to have been a winter camping area for local Indians, and artifacts have been found in the soil. I took my kids there years ago and they explored and found what we think were scrapers for hides. Some folks have found arrowheads. The area is quite overgrown now, but I think few realize that hill, clearly visible from the water, was an Indian winter encampment. The location makes sense.

To the north of Bantam Lake is a place they call Little Bantam. The ice fishing there used to be great. And around the pond and swamp is a wonderful boardwalk that is worth exploring – a naturalist's treat. On Windmill Hill is the White Memorial Foundation headquarters and museum. It's a great place, and one can get information and maps for exploring the many beautiful trails that surround the place. I have hiked and our family has cross-country skied many of the trails. It is an exhilarating area, and well worth the effort to explore. We liked the Cranberry Pond trail and the trail to Plunge Pool to the East. The White Memorial does a great job preserving these precious areas.

Chuckle 22

Ever see someone go to step out of a boat and on to the dock and they step between both?

Chapter 23

I Have Always Ice Fished!

Years ago our family went to the 1980 Winter Olympics. We stayed in a motel in Lake George, and were bused into Lake Placid to watch the ski jumping event. That was a thrill and a memorable experience for us all.

While staying in the area we had time on our hands so we decided to ice fish Lake George. I just happened to have a few pieces of equipment with me, and we headed out on the lake from the downtown "Fort" area.

There was a slip-sliding stock car race going on and people were parking north of us *on the ice*. We were impressed. The race cars had special tires that gripped the ice.

And we got a flag! Up through the "feet" of ice came a real nice three to four pound landlocked salmon. It was a nice fish, and a very pleasant surprise. The kids and I were quite impressed. We took a picture and released the fish.

The day culminated with a great happening, when the whole town of Lake George seemed to cheer all at once. The cheers could be heard coming from the village and echoed off the hills. The USA Olympic ice hockey team had defeated the Russian team. People were celebrating and honking horns everywhere. Parties began and a sense of pride permeated the whole town.

As years crept by I spent many winters on the ice. I often fished with John, and think I enjoyed ice fishing even as much as open water fishing. The cold and solitude were often refreshing and meeting the challenges gave me great satisfaction. When younger, I went out in all kinds of weather and sometimes the temperature and wind were a challenge. Temps of twenty below take careful planning. Good equipment and common sense rule, of course, and now that I am older and retired, I can pick the nice days.

Weather being acceptable, I figured out in short fashion the best day to ice fish. After retirement I avoided Saturday's and Sunday's, leaving the weekends for those folks that are working. Logic will tell you Monday is the day to ice fish. Safe tracks on the ice and snow can be seen, and if the temperature hasn't plunged too far, there are holes *everywhere* that are easy to open and use. For a jigging ice fisherman that moves around a lot, that's a great situation. By studying the old holes, and knowing one's hotspots, the scale begins to tip in one's favor. Mondays are great and this tip again is just between you and me!

John and I ice fished Mudge Pond on and off many times. A few years ago we decided to return to that peaceful place and chase panfish. We parked at the boat launch and had to walk a tricky path on land to find safe ice to enter the lake. We followed other's tracks going out and had a good day and we each caught enough to make a nice meal. When leaving the ice, John veered off track a bit toward a beaver lodge. Yep – crunch – and a wet foot came up again! We turned up the heater on the way home and John again vowed to send me ahead of him from now on. I was thankful for my luck so far.

John and I have spent many years on the ice. He would often build a fire (he loves fires), and many trips would see a stove hauled out too. I had (and still have) a one burner propane stove and John had a burner he called a "grasshopper". It looked like one when set up and we often heated soup, hot dogs, kielbasa, or hot chocolate. I know there are many people that truly enjoy a good day of cooking, fishing, and comradery under sunny winter skies. Add a couple of youngsters, or perhaps a dog, and great fun follows. As they say, it doesn't get any better.

As I got older, I of course got wiser. Although I have started taking less and less, we were always safety conscious, John even more than me. I started carrying two screwdrivers in my pockets, to use as ice picks if I needed them to pull myself out of the ice. And I started wearing a life jacket. Although looking a bit silly, I did feel safer. As a bonus it keeps me very warm, too. Even today, if any doubt or not, I take a life jacket and a long rope is always a must, too. One never knows if it will be needed, and it could save a life.

One should also know the lake being fished, and take nothing for granted. Thin ice is nothing to fool with. We often bought Massachusetts licenses just because, in the western part of the state, the ice was thicker longer. Elevation was a factor.

Mentioned earlier, we fished Lower Moodus frequently. John (more than I) often talked to other fishermen on our outings and we became quite enamored with a fellow who fished with his son. The boy was about eight or nine years old, and loved ice fishing. They would scamper out from the boat launch on Lower Moodus and stop, talk, and continue on their way. The man put in holes and tip-ups and his son, on his knees more than not, fished avidly. His mom or someone dressed him warmly, but every trip, he seemed to get his knees soaked, looking down holes or whatever. Time and again, he got soaked. He loved fishing, and his dad never stayed long enough for him to get cold. "Mr. Wet Knees" never complained and if memory serves me right, over time, John gave them some extra equipment he had. It was great to see such a father/son combination.

Part of the charm of the sport is meeting people and "characters" that also love the sport. As I have "aged", I have become less reclusive. I have met several notable characters that have taught me just a little bit more.

One fellow I met was "Bluegill Bob". I met him a few years ago on Tyler Lake ice fishing for gills. He went by Bluegill Bob, and I think he was quite proud of the nickname. He was an older fellow and had a nice sled setup. He sat on a bucket in his sled, and had a nice wall of sorts to break the wind, should it come up. He had a favorite "spot" off the boat launch, and was a friendly fellow. His tiny lures were homemade and he even gave me one. And he had a special sauce he had prepared. Now, don't read this out loud! The sauce he soaked his bait (and lures) in was anise and sawdust, mixed to a damp consistency. And he caught bluegills!

Bob smoked a pipe and as he moved around a bit, he would light and smoke. After he left, John and I could always find his most productive hole by seeing where the most ashes were. I saw his picture in the local paper one spring, fishing at Black Rock Pond. He was sitting in the rain by the shore under an umbrella, and the words "Bluegill Bob" were in the caption! I haven't seen him lately, but I always keep an eye open for him when I'm on the ice.

As I got older, the power auger got heavier for me. With a hiatal hernia bugging me, I opted for a five inch Lazer auger. It met my ice drilling needs well, and was light to carry. The power auger was sold to some lucky young fellow at our tag sale. It was fun to watch him talk his girlfriend into the *great need* for buying it.

Around 2008, I met another fellow on Tyler Lake that intrigued me. As I watched him ice fish, I noticed how easily he drilled holes in the ice. I used my Lazer auger, and it worked fine, but this fellow had it down even better. I wandered over and started a conversation. He was a panfisherman and introduced himself as Charlie, and I could see he, too, was a tinkerer. He had some cool stuff going on. For one thing, he had cut old pill bottles in such a way that they fit over the lures on the end of his poles. With a slit in the plastic bottles they were capped with the lures inside. They could not get hooked into anything by mistake, and were safe as can be- a great idea.

I then asked him about drilling holes, and he very graciously showed me a gizmo called the Ice Master (icemasteradapter.com). It pins onto the lower part of the auger, and allows one to put the other end into a drill chuck – yes, a drill chuck. Charlie had a portable battery-powered heavy-duty drill attached to his auger. He graciously showed me how it worked and explained that one needed a drill with at least four hundred inch pounds of torque to be effective. He drilled holes effortlessly!

I bought a drill! Sears had a hammer drill on sale with four hundred and twenty inch pounds of torque and two 19.2 V batteries. I have since bought several more batteries. With about eleven inches of ice, and a drill attached to my Lazer auger, I can drill twelve to thirteen five inch holes on each battery – effortlessly! I keep the spare batteries warm in an insulated lunch bag with an activated hand warmer or a plastic jar of hot water. Thanks to Charlie, an old fellow like me can continue to drill holes and keep moving. Watch out panfish!

On an earlier trip to Garfield Lake, John and I were very entertained when a young dapper couple came out from shore to see what we were doing ice fishing. This was a novelty to the young lady, who happened to be from New York City. John showed her how the manual auger worked, and she was just awed and tickled to be able to drill holes. We were fascinated with her new found interest, and holes she did drill!

At another time when we were on the ice at Hayward Lake, we met another young couple out for some serious bass fishing. The fellow told us he had caught some big bass previously on big minnows (just below the ice). They moved down the lake they were setting up tip-ups in the distance, and getting ready to fish. As the lady went to sit down on their five gallon bucket – plop – over backward she went into the snow, her feet straight up in the air! Not a *graceful* move. We nicknamed her Grace! For some reason, we found that quite amusing.

And we don't just meet people. Tyler Lake has a dog that lives just beside the launch. He looks, watches, and nods okay every time I launch or ice fish! No barking, just peacefully guarding his turf and enjoying the activities (and I know his master is a fisherman, too).

On Garfield Lake in Massachusetts, there once lived "Bear". No, not a bear, but a dog named Bear. Bear would watch fishermen come onto the ice from his red cottage. They (and we) would set up and in no time, this big black dog would nonchalantly wander onto the ice. Now, it's pretty hard for a big black dog to go unnoticed on the white snowy ice, but bear thought no one could see him as he zigged and zagged his way to our ice sleds. It was fun to watch, as he hoped to discover a grinder or a ham sandwich that might be unattended. We had to watch our lures (could have used Charlie's inventions) as he snooped around, got petted, and wandered off to the next party realizing we were on to him. We put Snausages and dog cookies on our list of things to bring. Meeting these different characters really brings another dimension to the sport!

I am always anxious to get out ice fishing, and I check around quite often at the beginning of the season. Any time I can start before Christmas seems to be a bonus.

In 2009, on January 3, I decided to check the ice on Tyler Lake. Tyler, because of its elevation, seems to freeze up before other lakes. I took a manual auger (no drill) and one bucket and pole just too quickly check out the lake. I was only checking! When I arrived, I was delighted; there were a few fishermen on the lake. Impatient, I headed out anyway just to check.

The lake had a dusting of snow, maybe a half-inch. I carefully walked out on the slippery ice and checked someone else's predrilled hole and found six inches of ice. Out I went toward the middle. Everything was safe and near the middle of the lake, I paused, and decided to fish for just a minute. I drilled a hole, and took one more step and, wham; I slipped on the powder-covered ice and went down sideways with a thump, falling on the auger. When the stars went away the sky was pretty, but I couldn't get up or move for a while!! I had pain! I finally got up enough to sit on the bucket and knew something was wrong. Breathing was difficult. Embarrassed, although other fishermen were far off, I tried to catch my breath.

"Mr. Stupid" had gone out on the ice without ice cleats on his feet. I was pretty sure I had broken ribs. I finally stood up, thought about how far away the van was, and balanced as best I could. With the bucket and pole in one hand and the auger in the other, and walking like a penguin, I took shuffle baby steps for about a quarter of a mile. It was a long walk off that ice and I thought I would be toast if I fell again!

I made it of course, and had a difficult drive home. The emergency room confirmed two fractured ribs, and I didn't dare sneeze for weeks. So much for not wearing ice cleats! It was four weeks before I got out again that season. I do keep a journal of trips, and recorded the next trip at the end of that January.

Chuckle 23

When my wife thinks I'm a loon, is it a compliment to me or is she "dishing" the loon?

Tyler Lake, Goshen, CT

Chapter 24

Quirky Stuff

I too, like Charlie, liked to tinker with or adapt things. Here are some ideas that may prove useful to some.

Most of the time, I pull two six foot plastic toboggans onto the ice, but they sometimes get very tippy in snow. John bought one of those nice wider black sleds in 2010, and it works well (Bluegill Bob had one).But I improvised. I cut two aluminum tent poles to the right length and tied them across my sleds through holes drilled in the edges. With good rope and tight knots, they worked great, like a one piece "raft". They have become extremely stable.

When catching fish on the ice, especially panfish, sometimes one wants to cull them. Therefore, I use a bucket instead of a reservoir in the ice, since we move a lot. That allows me to throw some back if I wish. The problem was how to get water into the bucket. To solve that problem, I took a small diameter dowel and duct- taped a larger plastic peanut butter jar to the end of it. It fits down a five inch hole perfectly and I can get water easily with not too many dips! Watching me, they may call me a dip!! And a bucket of water will hold a pole over a hole and its weight will keep the sleds from blowing away.

I also taped a dowel onto the plastic scoop to clear the hole. The older I get, the farther away the ice gets. I don't have to bend as far now.

When John and I ice fish, we often stay till just about dark. We have had a hard time seeing the clear monofilament line as the sun goes down. John got some red line and it showed up better against the snow. Having an idea about this, I went to my cellar, got out a permanent red marker, and ran it up and down my clear monofilament. I skipped the first five feet. It works great, and the line not marked is used down the hole attached to the lure. The red "magic marker" line shows up extremely well, even in dim light.

PVC pipe is great stuff. Using electrical tape, I taped eight inch pieces of one inch pipe to the side of nine inch blocks of 2X4's. In deeper ice, they slip into a five inch hole perfectly. When I make the hole, I don't break through the bottom of the hole. The PVC pipe will then allow one to slip aluminum tent poles into them. Another block with a horseshoe nail can slip into another hole to allow a rope to hold the tent pole. With some clamps, one can then put up a wind wall with a small tarp-warm, warm, warm!

A piece of one and a half inch PVC pipe taped to a bucket can also hold an umbrella. All our umbrellas have a hole drilled into the handle (my poor wife). By putting a bolt through the PVC and the handle, one has protection from drizzle and snow! I also have two 31 inch pieces of PVC for the boat. I screwed one-and-a-half inch caps onto the floor of the boat near the seats. When needed the PVC fits into the cap, the umbrella and bolt fits into the top of the PVC, and I have a quick shelter for showers, or protection from the sun with an umbrella over my head. Bungee cords secure the pipe.

For those of you with cold feet, we found that the thick rubber ice cleats keep feet warm because one is off the ice. Putting one's feet on a 2 foot piece of board will do the same thing.

I once came across some chewing tobacco canisters. I decided to try a few for holding bait. I drilled tiny holes in the lids, washed them out, and painted the tops different colors. They are great for mealworms, mousies, and wax worms and they don't crush in your pocket – great bait containers. They also store in the fridge well.

In the summer, I often take a radio with me fishing. No, I don't listen to it, I use it. If one puts the radio on a non-station, you can hear lightning miles away! It makes a good early warning system, and lightning gets louder as the storm approaches.

I love a product called Goop. I end up with wrist watches that have broken wrist bands. I take the bands off and put a dot of goop on the back. Then I glue it to the side of my boat. The time is there, and usually the watch lasts for a couple of years.

I wore out the prow of my small boat pulling it ashore over the years. The sand and shore caused me to have to patch that prow. Learning a lesson, on my "newer" boat, I squirt Goop on the prow every spring. It has protected it ever since!

I know many fishing poles have hook- keepers where one can hook a lure to a pole when not using the pole. I have found that a small piece of florists wire (the fine wire used for making wreaths) looped around the spinning reel shaft makes a real good place to hook one's lures. The lure is better protected by the pole on top and the reel body on the bottom, keeping it well out of reach of most snags.

When I got my sixteen foot boat, I noticed I had trouble hitching the launch rope and the winch rope to the same ring on the front bow. I solved that problem by putting a second ring a few inches over the original one. Now, with two rings, I have no problem.

I use a lot of different lures, but jigs are a favorite. I don't like to admit it, but I have more fingernail polish than my wife. Whoa! Yep, I paint jig heads and lures. This past summer I caught a landlocked salmon on a Sutton spoon painted hot pink. The little jig heads I use are painted with glitter nail polish with black dots for eyes. And you should see what I have done to some Mooseluk Wobblers – decorated with all kinds of spots and stripes. For my next experiment I am going to try a glow-in-the-dark paint. I found a small bottle at a tag sale and got some great ideas. Some of my ice jigs will be "glowing" in the dark, and I may try it with some of the other lures too.

I have had some success with free standing jigging pole holders on the ice. Usually, one doesn't catch much with a motionless jigging pole. But often times the wind blows. You know those address labels one gets free in the mail, the peel off kind? Well, sometimes there are bigger ones, almost the size of a business card. I took some with me on the ice and stuck them to the rod tip of a motionless free standing pole. Yep, the wind wiggled the rod tip, and a few bites ensued! Give it a try.

We also have saved a lot of money using instant glue to glue tubes onto the heads of the jigs. The tubes last almost five times longer, and the glue dries in just minutes.

Just recently, I stumbled onto an idea to keep my boots warm till I get to the frozen lake. I used to put them under the van heater on the way. Now, I just fill two liter soda bottles with hot tap water and shove them into my boots. When I put them on at the lake, they are toasty warm.

Well, so much for some quirks and gizmos. I haven't yet figured out how to activate bottle rockets with tip-up flags, but I just might try. That would be cool!

I still have places and lakes to explore. But I really just enjoy the challenge of visiting *familiar* places and trying something slightly different or radically upside down. It's fun to hear, "What are you using," or "You caught that on what?" And I love going back to the good ol' lures once in a while. Last year I saw a big northern caught on a Jitterbug casted from shore.

And I make lists now. It comes with age – I like to call it fermenting. And don't tell me you haven't forgotten something – like lunch, the bait, or the camera! I decided I didn't like forgetting, so I made two basic master lists that I always check before leaving the house. I don't always need everything, but at least I have a "reminder list" to keep me on track. I even back the list up the night before with sticky pad notes either on the cooler or the steering wheel. One list is for ice fishing, the other for open water. Perhaps they will be useful to you (when you get older). Of course not all these things are needed and some things can stay in the car or truck. I often carry blankets and an extra snowmobile suit or some clothes in case someone needs emergency help. The same goes for the first aid kit. I have found that if I am diligent enough to check the list, my day goes very well.

Open Water List

License	Bucket
Depth finder	Fire extinguisher
Net	Fingernail clippers
Lunch	Belt pliers
Bait	Binoculars
Poles	Camera
Life preserver	Pills(aspirin,antacids,etc)
Electric motor/battery	Dark glasses
Radio	Fingerless gloves (for sun)
Tackle boxes	Rain gear
Sun block	Hat
Umbrella	Towel/rags
Boots (for launching)	"P" bucket
Phone	Flashlight
Launch rope	First aid kit
Sun hat	Band-Aids

Ice Fishing List

Poles

License

Bait

Warm clothes bucket

Gloves

Lures

Fish bucket

Auger/+drill

Sleds

Rope/boat cushion

Pics for around neck/or screw drivers

Depth finder/small battery

Bungees (to hold stuff!)

Boots/spikes

Sun glasses

Camera

Pills(aspirin, antacids,etc)

Binoculars

Lifejacket

Lunch

Thermos

Fingernail clipper

Belt pliers

First aid kit

Band-Aids

Sunblock

Towel/rag

Flashlight

Phone

Shovel/sand

Chuckle 24

When one goes "tooling" down the highway to get fishing, why are half the boat cushions missing at the launch?

Chapter 25

Contemplations

Every once in a while some new technique or lure comes along and I am surprised or delighted. Well, I'm still learning to fish. I guess I'll always be doing so. But as I slow down, my mind still streams ahead.

John and I were quite inspired years back when we met a couple of eighty-plus year old guys, ice fishing in Massachusetts. They bantered back and forth and were really enjoying the day. I think they introduced us to wax worms. I hope I will be as lucky and blessed with good health and spirit as those fellows.

As I looked over my lures I had a chuckle of a thought. I think someone could write a heck of a soap opera story using lure names for one's characters. The Rebel could be cheating on the Redeye Wiggler with the Hula Popper. Enter the Teardrop! At the same time the Crazy Crawler gang could be fighting with the Daredevils! Rat Finke could be their leader! And how do we control those Wiggle Warts? Well, so much for silliness!

Football may have its "Hail Mary's", tennis may have "love fifteen" or "love thirty", and golf has its "birdies" and "eagles", but fishing has its "homeruns" too! The lift of a blue heron from the glassy shallows, the thrill of the sight of one's first "real" eagle, and the fog rising with the sunrise all imprint nature onto our memories. Out there one hears the kingfisher's chatter looking for minnows, and not much beats the dive of an osprey catching a fish. The quack of duck, the call of the crow, and the squirt of fish under the boat as the sun peeks up in the morning just makes one feel alive. The territorial call of the red winged blackbird enhances the symphony. It does get addictive and of course there's the hunt!

And out on the ice it is ironic that the solitude lets us know that we are not alone.

In the course of daily adult life, I often had little time to fish. Kids' schedules, family obligations, and two jobs kept me busy. But when the opportunity popped up, the sport called me out. Whatever the weather, I would fish. Only lightning would keep me off the lake and it was often quite rewarding to challenge the elements successfully!

I've sat in a boat loaded with snow, challenged whitecaps everywhere, and ice fished in -20° weather with wind. Nothing can beat the satisfaction of meeting those challenges, of pretending your admiral Byrd, exploring the North Pole or something. Eyebrows covered with snow or huddling under a straw hat in the heat of the sun, nothing beats enjoying the great natural world. It is very hard to explain the peace one feels, alone on the ice, sitting on a bucket, reflecting, in a light snow. It tends to be a mind cleansing, cathartic event. To some of us the act of fishing is our church. It builds confidence and character as we grow up, knowing one can successfully meet challenges, and still perhaps "bring home the bacon" to boot. It's fun. It's addictive. And the comradery of friendships winds a golden thread through it all.

I am but a little splash in a great big pool of fishermen that really know their stuff. But fishing has definitely made me a better and stronger man, and given me untouchables I can't explain. It has humbled me and made me realize we are all surrounded by some precious gifts.

There is no better sleeping pill than lying in bed trying to figure out why the fish didn't bite, or wondering what could have been done better. Should I have fished deeper, or faster, or shallower, whatever? It sure beats worrying about things we can't change.

At some point, one realizes that fishing is not just the catching of fish. It's rejuvenation, decompression, and a general awe at what surrounds us. Fishermen soak in the sun rises, enjoy friendships, and claim the sparkles on the water as their gold. Even the first start of an outboard in the spring stirs our senses. Fishing is a wonderful sport that will lead down unexpected and delightful side roads.

The sport takes us away for awhile, but it returns us truly grounded in what counts. If one brings the right things to it, it will give us something special in return. I still feel that childish anticipation before each planned excursion. I'm more mature now but I'm still learning. And I still have more lakes to explore.

I have had the most enjoyable time chasing the ghosts we call fish and the spirits that inhabit every sunrise, every drizzle, every fish that breaks water. I thank the good Lord for every trip, every discovery. And one of these days, I will have learned how to fish, but school is still in session!

Get Out There

No more can I fish,
As I have in the past,
And fewer the days
Between me and the last.

For the nights are long,
And the days grow dark,
And life has left
It's indelible mark.

But out on the lakes,
And up-and-down streams,
I carry my thoughts,
I carry my dreams.

Of course I fish,
And still I ponder,
The wonderful world
That's way out yonder.

Get out there folks,
Enjoy the sun,
And wonder the world
That God has spun!